GOD, I NEED Some Answers

LIFE LESSONS *from* PSALMS

David Jeremiah

P.O. Box 3838
San Diego, CA 92163

Edited by Jordan Davis

Unless otherwise indicated, Scripture verses quoted are taken from the NEW KING JAMES VERSION.

Printed in the United States of America.

CONTENTS

About Dr. David Jeremiah and Turning Point

Dr. David Jeremiah is the founder of Turning Point, a ministry committed to providing Christians with sound Bible teaching relevant to today's changing times through radio and television broadcasts, audio series, books, and live events. Dr. Jeremiah's common-sense teaching on topics such as family, prayer, worship, angels, and biblical prophecy forms the foundation of Turning Point.

David and his wife, Donna, reside in El Cajon, California, where he serves as the senior pastor of Shadow Mountain Community Church. David and Donna have four children and twelve grandchildren.

In 1982, Dr. Jeremiah brought the same solid teaching to San Diego television that he shares weekly with his congregation. Shortly thereafter, Turning Point expanded its ministry to radio. Dr. Jeremiah's inspiring messages can now be heard worldwide on radio, television, and the Internet.

Because Dr. Jeremiah desires to know his listening audience, he travels nationwide holding ministry rallies and spiritual enrichment conferences that touch the hearts and lives of many people. According to Dr. Jeremiah, "At some point in time, everyone reaches a turning point; and for every person, that moment is unique, an experience to hold onto forever. There's so much changing in today's world that sometimes it's difficult to choose the right path. Turning Point offers people an understanding of God's Word as well as the opportunity to make a difference in their lives."

Dr. Jeremiah has authored numerous books, including ***Escape the Coming Night*** (Revelation), ***The Handwriting on the Wall*** (Daniel), ***Overcoming Loneliness, Prayer—The Great Adventure, God in You*** (Holy Spirit), ***When Your World Falls Apart, Slaying the Giants in Your Life, My Heart's Desire, Sanctuary, Captured by Grace, Signs of Life, God Loves You: He Always Has—He Always Will, What Are You Afraid Of?, Agents of the Apocalypse, Overcomer, The Book of Signs,*** **and** ***The Jesus You May Not Know.***

About This Study Guide

The purpose of this Turning Point study guide is to reinforce Dr. David Jeremiah's dynamic, in-depth teaching and to aid the reader in applying biblical truth to his or her daily life. This study guide is designed to be used in conjunction with Dr. Jeremiah's *God, I Need Some Answers* audio series, but it may also be used by itself for personal or group study.

Structure of the Lessons

Each lesson is based on one of the messages in the *God, I Need Some Answers* compact disc series and focuses on specific passages in the Bible. Each lesson is composed of the following elements:

• *Outline*

The outline at the beginning of the lesson gives a clear, concise picture of the topic being studied and provides a helpful framework for readers as they listen to Dr. Jeremiah's teaching.

• *Overview*

The overview summarizes Dr. Jeremiah's teaching on the passage being studied in the lesson. Readers should refer to the Scripture passages in their own Bibles as they study the overview. Unless otherwise indicated, Scripture verses quoted are taken from the New King James Version.

• *Application*

This section contains a variety of questions designed to help readers dig deeper into the lesson and the Scriptures, and to apply the lesson to their daily lives. For Bible study groups or Sunday school classes, these questions will provide a springboard for group discussion and interaction.

• *Did You Know?*

This section presents a fascinating fact, historical note, or insight that adds a point of interest to the preceding lesson.

Using This Guide for Group Study

The lessons in this study guide are suitable for Sunday school classes, small-group studies, elective Bible studies, or home Bible study groups. Each person in the group should have his or her own study guide.

When possible, the study guide should be used with the corresponding compact disc series. You may wish to assign the study guide lesson as homework prior to the meeting of the group and then use the meeting time to listen to the CD and discuss the lesson.

For Continuing Study

For a complete listing of Dr. Jeremiah's materials for personal and group study call 1-800-947-1993, go online to www.DavidJeremiah.org, or write to: Turning Point, P.O. Box 3838, San Diego, CA 92163.

Dr. Jeremiah's *Turning Point* program is currently heard or viewed around the world on radio, television, and the Internet in English. *Momento Decisivo*, the Spanish translation of Dr. Jeremiah's messages, can be heard on radio in every Spanish speaking country in the world. The television broadcast is also broadcast by satellite throughout the Middle East with Arabic subtitles.

Contact Turning Point for radio and television program times and stations in your area. Or visit our website at www.DavidJeremiah.org.

God, I Need Some Answers

INTRODUCTION

Sometimes it is easy to feel like we just don't measure up to the heroes of the Bible—those men and women who so faithfully served God with their entire being. Think of Abraham and Noah and Moses. Think of the trust that they placed in God. It is easy to become discouraged when we compare our lives to theirs. They were so godly and God-fearing that sometimes they don't even seem real.

But that is only on the surface, for the Bible reveals the full portrait of these men. And although they were men of great faith, they too were fallible. Abraham became impatient with God's timing and disobediently bore a son through Hagar (Genesis 16). After God delivered Noah and his family through the flood, Noah dishonored God by becoming drunk (Genesis 9:21). And Moses not only killed a man (Exodus 2:12), but he argued so much with God that God became angry (Exodus 4:14).

So it's good to know that even the men whom God used in great ways to establish His Kingdom had failures and struggles just like the rest of us. And no one personifies this more than David.

David was a poet, warrior, musician, and king. A man for the ages. A man after God's own heart (Acts 13:22). Truly, if there was ever to be a man who would fully embody wisdom, consistency, and stability regarding the things of the Lord, it would be David.

Yet, David experienced spiritual failure. He committed adultery and murder. And there were great consequences to these sins. But there is also great comfort in knowing that even a man who was set apart and desired to follow God (and through whose lineage Christ would be born) had great struggles in his life. And we can benefit from his experience because we have his writings.

Many of the Psalms were written by David. They encompass the highest of highs and lowest of lows. Moments of great praise and adulation and moments of despair and doubt. And God saw fit to record these supplications that welled up in his heart and spirit.

And when we read and analyze these Scriptures that God in His wisdom preserved for us in His Word, we can garner how best we are to live our lives in a pleasing and honoring way to Him.

David had questions and frustrations just like the rest of us. And though thousands of years span our time from his, the questions remain the same. Questions of identity—like who am I and what is my self-worth? Questions of direction—such as how do I face my fears and how can I champion my family? And questions of faith—like why do the wicked prosper and how can my sins be forgiven?

The purpose of *God, I Need Some Answers—Life Lessons from Psalms* is to do just that: to give you God's eternal perspective on the questions that are universal to mankind. Isn't it good to know that God does not leave us comfortless? In addition to the work of the Holy Spirit, He has given us His Word. But to benefit from it, we have to read it! So prayerfully and carefully use this study guide to plumb the depths of the Psalms. God will reward you—and you will find the answers you have been looking for.

WHO AM I AND WHY AM I HERE?

Psalm 8

In this lesson we will discover where answers to life's most important questions can be found.

OUTLINE

One doesn't have to be a philosopher to ask life's deepest questions. Everyone wrestles with identity and purpose in life, and people reach varying conclusions in their search. But the most satisfying answers are those found in the Creator, in creation, and in Christ.

I. Answers Found in the Creator
- A. We Know God Through His Transcendent Creation
- B. We Know God Through His Personal Communication

II. Answers Found in Creation
- A. God's Original Intention
- B. Our Fallen Condition

III. Answers Found in Christ
- A. Christ Recovers Our Innocence
- B. Christ Recovers Our Eternal Life

OVERVIEW

In the beginning of his life, H. G. Wells had an incredibly positive view of mankind. His early writings contained the belief that "Our race will more than realize our boldest imaginations." He believed peace and unity were forthcoming; he envisioned a utopian world. But World War I punctured his philosophy of optimism like a pin punctures a balloon. Especially after the beginning of World War II, H. G. Wells's writings became dark, dismal, and discouraging. Despair was written over everything. As he came to the end of his life, he could hardly remember that earlier he had been an apostle of positive thinking in his day.

Life has a way of doing that to many of us. We start out with hopes and dreams, and then life settles in. If we aren't plugged in to the right circuits along the way, we can become the epitome of everything we preached against in our early years. Trying to come to grips with the meaning of life can cause despair if the questioner cannot come up with any meaningful answers.

When I read David's question, "What is man that You are mindful of him, and the son of man that You visit him?" (Psalm 8:4), I don't want to know just what the question is, but what the answer means. There are three important truths that we need to write down in the table of our heart if we are going to come to grips with that answer. These critical points will help us to understand who we are and why we are here.

Answers Found in the Creator

You cannot understand who you are and why you are here until you understand the Creator. The theme of Psalm 8 blazes across the first and last verses of this hymn. "O Lord, our Lord, how excellent is Your name in all the earth!" Human meaning begins and ends with the glory of God and who He is.

What makes people different from every other created work on earth? "God created man in His own image" (Genesis 1:27). When God created people, He created them to respond to God. God possesses intellect, emotion, and will; and He created people with intellect, emotion, and will so that He could walk in the garden with the first people and talk with them and commune with them. No other creature knows that kind of intimate, personal fellowship with God in heaven. And so it is true to say that man is only man in relationship to God.

We Know God Through His Transcendent Creation

We can know our Creator through His created works. The handiwork of God is beautiful—putting the stars in the sky, hanging the moon and the sun. Who has not looked up at the sky and thought about the grandeur and majesty of our God?

We Know God Through His Personal Communication

God is known to us in His transcendent creation, but He is also known to us in His personal communication. In verse two, "Out of the mouth of babes and nursing infants You have ordained strength, because of Your enemies, that You may silence the enemy and the avenger." What impressed the psalmist was that this transcendent glory of God, this greatness which was far above all the heavens, could still be grasped and expressed by a child. David had often struggled to put his words into thoughts and ideas and had found that his intelligence and rationality were challenged by such an attempt. Yet this same God who can overwhelm us by revealing Himself in the star-studded heavens can be known in the heart of a child.

Jesus nailed this truth for us in Matthew. Jesus had been healing the blind and lame in the temple. When the chief priests saw this and heard the children shouting, "Hosanna to the Son of David," they got upset. These children weren't a trained children's temple choir. They were the ragamuffins of the street. And the chief priests and scribes thought Jesus should be offended that these street urchins were crying out, "Hosanna to the Son of David!" But Jesus reminded them of this particular psalm and said, "Out of the mouth of babes and nursing infants You have perfected praise" (Matthew 21:15-16).

God is so magnificent—He created the world and hung the stars—yet the simplest child can comprehend Him. In fact, simple children understand Him better than we do once we get our minds messed up with the intricacies of life.

Ken Poure tells a story about his granddaughter who was about eight at the time. He and his granddaughter were talking about God, and he asked her, "What do you like about God?" She thought about it for a minute and then she said, "You know what I like about God? God never says, 'Oops!'" Isn't it incredible that a child could understand the perfection of Almighty God?

Out of the mouths of babes come little words of challenge, like the questions from the child who said, "Why don't we have a Bible? Will you buy me a Bible?" Or the statement to the father who never prayed, that it was daddy's turn to pray. If we've written down the memoirs of our family, our notebooks would be full of illustrations like that.

Answers Found in Creation

You cannot know who you are and why you are here until you come to know your Creator. You also cannot know who you are and why you are here until you understand creation. The answer to the second part of the question is—you are here to subdue the earth. Psalm 8:6 says, "You have made him to have dominion over the works of Your hands; You have put all things under his feet." Psalm 8 is a commentary on what God intended humankind to be.

God's Original Intention

Hebrews 2 tells us what happened to God's original intention. God wanted people to live in the Garden of Eden, in control over the animal kingdom just as they were king of the earth—God's sovereign creation ruling in sovereign control over all creation. But humankind wanted more. The only thing God withheld was withheld in order that they might remember who God was and that they were not God. But they took hold of the forbidden thing and caused what we call the Fall. Man was divested of all opportunity to rule over the animal kingdom.

Our Fallen Condition

Our relationship to creation is evidence of our lost sovereignty. In our fallen condition, as we try to rule and reign over the earth, we build factories to provide jobs for people and goods for nations, but the factories pollute the waters of our streams and lakes. We take the money we make at the factories and buy automobiles to make it easier to get to work, and the automobiles fill the air with poisonous gases. Our eyes burn and our lungs are clogged with smog. Trying to do right, we do wrong because we have lost our sovereignty in creation.

You will never understand who you are and why you are here until you understand that. Why is the world in the mess it's in? Because Adam rebelled against the almighty God. That's why if you love God and want to serve Him and make a difference in this world, you discover there are bumps in the road. That's why Scripture says the whole creation groans until the day of redemption (see Romans 8:22).

Answers Found in Christ

We've lost our sovereignty, and we're living in a fallen world. Something had to be done. Hebrews tells us what it is: "But we see Jesus, who was made a little lower than the angels, for the suffering of death crowned with glory and honor, that He, by the grace of God, might taste death for everyone" (Hebrews 2:9).

If you compare this verse to Psalm 8:5–8, you will discover that the same terms are used to describe Jesus in Hebrews 2 as are used of mankind in the psalm. What was lost through the first Adam has been recovered through the "second Adam," Jesus Christ. Christ walked into this world and took back the control that was lost when Adam sinned. In other words, Christ started a new humanity. He started a whole new race of people called "redeemed," who have been caught up out of the brokenness of this world and set up on a new level that makes sense and puts meaning into every day. He has a plan for your life. Christ has recovered everything that was lost in the Garden of Eden for those who put their trust in Him.

Christ Recovers Our Innocence

What was lost in the Garden? Man's innocence and eternal life. Jesus entered our world as a baby and left as a man. He came to recover the things that were lost in the sin of the Garden of Eden. He went to the Cross. There He let all the sin of the world come down upon Him, and the wrath of God poured on Him—the sinless Son of God. He takes away all the penalty of our sin when we put our trust in Him so that we can recover the sense of purity and innocence in Jesus Christ.

Christ Recovers Our Eternal Life

The Scripture says when Jesus died, He took the sting out of death. He took the poison away and emptied death of its sting. The message of hope and encouragement is that the grave is not the end, the sting of death is momentary and there is life everlasting.

When Jesus grew up on this earth, He demonstrated everything we could be in Christ, even in the physical realm. Jesus turned water into wine. He told a storm to be still and it was still. The miracles He did, He did as a man—the Son of Man who had control over nature.

He was demonstrating again for us everything God had originally wanted us to have that was lost in the Garden through sin. He was reminding us that someday in the kingdom the lion will lie down with the lamb and there will be peace between humanity and the animal kingdom. Someday we will once again have dominion over the living things.

It is through Jesus Christ that we can recover the sense of who we are and why we are here. We can never understand or recover it in any other way. When we put our faith in Jesus Christ, we allow Him to be our representative even as Adam was in the Old Testament. He paid the penalty for our sin and sets us free from the prison house of our human desires, and offers us the opportunity to understand what life is all about.

Insight into who you are and why you are here is available only from the Creator because you were created for Him. The missing piece in your life is not more education or better therapy. The missing piece in your life, if you don't know Christ, is to put Him at the center where He belongs. God created you uniquely for Himself. He put a vacuum within you that cannot be filled with anything else but Him. When you stuff in all the pleasure and all the madness of this age, trying to find meaning to life, you will never discover it. But something happens when you say a simple prayer, giving in to God and receiving Him into your life.

Then Jesus comes to live within you. Your problems are not gone, but you have a new understanding, a new perspective, a new sense of purpose, and a new sense of meaning. Life starts to make sense. The rest of your life as a believer is the gradual awareness day in and day out of who you are in Christ and what God intends for your life.

God loves you, He knows you, He has a plan for your life. He wants you to know who you are and why you are here; and if you will put your trust in Him, He will give you that perspective in your life. You were created in God's image, so you are really only yourself in relationship to God. When you let God take control of your life through His Son, life begins to have meaning.

APPLICATION

1. Read Genesis 1:26–31.

   a. God made man according to what two aspects of Himself? (verse 26a)

   b. With such knowledge of how we are made, what should a Christian's attitude be toward the sanctity of human life at all levels?

   c. God graciously gave man dominion over what five things? (verse 26b)

      1.

      2.

      3.

      4.

      5.

   d. What is reiterated not once but twice in verse 27? Why is this such an important point to understand when considering our purpose in life?

e. In addition to repeating that which man has dominion over, God gives man two specific commands in verse 28. What are they?

f. Do you think those commands given in verse 28 still apply to us today? Why or why not?

g. In verse 29, God declares that He has given man what? For what purpose?

h. God provides not only for the needs of man but also for the needs of what other creatures? (verse 30)

i. When God viewed all He had made and all the preparations He made for creation, what was His conclusion? (verse 31)

j. What should be our conclusion when we consider the detail shown in God's handiwork of our creation?

2. Read Psalm 8.

a. Out of what unlikely source has God ordained strength? (verse 2) What does this tell you about the nature of God?

b. What things are described as the work of God's fingers? (verse 3) What does this tell you about the power of God?

c. In light of this power, what is God mindful of? (verse 4) What does this tell about the purpose of God?

d. Verses 6-8 reiterate much of what is said in what verse in Genesis chapter 1?

e. What is the psalmist's conclusion to the works and ways of God? (verse 9)

3. In light of these two passages of Scripture, what can you say with certainty about the life that God has given you?

DID YOU KNOW?

The complexity of God's creation is truly staggering. It is hard to comprehend all that God has put into place: the rotation of the earth, gravity, the orbits of the planets, the vast and unknown universe itself. And earth alone is filled with a plethora of different ecosystems that contain so much animal and plant life, that we are still discovering new species to this very day. But all these things are diminutive in comparison to God because Psalm 8:3 tells us all created things are merely the work of His fingers!

What Is My Self-Worth?

Psalm 139

In this lesson you will discover why God's opinion of you is the most important opinion of all.

OUTLINE

As children we learn to be overly concerned about what others think of us. Sometimes our self-worth rises when we hear from others, and other times it plummets. Maintaining a proper view of self is best accomplished by valuing God's opinion above all others.

I. God Knows You

A. God Knows What You Do
B. God Knows What You Think
C. God Knows Where You Go
D. God Knows What You Say
E. God Knows What You Need

II. God Is Near You

III. God Made You

A. God Protects Your Individuality
B. God Protects Your Identity
C. God Protects Your Importance

IV. God Is Thinking of You

OVERVIEW

Countless thousands of people are spending thousands of dollars for therapy and counseling to find out who they are, why they are here, and whether they are worthy—trying to discover their self-worth and find a reason for continuing the struggle just to keep going. Because of today's evolutionary theory, many people accept that we are a tiny speck in the vast universe. We're struggling mortals on an obscure planet located in a second-rate galaxy among billions of other galaxies. So how important can we really be? In our western culture, we've decided that the worth of a person is determined on the basis of how much society is willing to pay for his services.

In the athletic world, it's not the worth of the person we applaud, it's how much we can get from him in terms of applause and how much we're willing to pay him. In the corporate world, the visible symbols of wealth and power announce the worth of a person. In the military, stripes and uniforms and the chain of command alert everyone to a person's worth. Throughout our culture, physical appearance and defining achievements decide how we rate each other.

Some years back in the *British Journal of Plastic Surgery,* there was a disturbing article called "The Quasimodo Complex." Two physicians surveyed 11,000 inmates who had committed murder, rape, or other serious crimes. In the normal adult population, twenty percent of all people have surgically correctable facial deformities like protruding ears, a misshapen nose, receding chins, acne scars, and birth marks. In the inmate population that was surveyed, sixty percent of the inmates had those kinds of deformities. The article ended with the question—Had these criminals encountered hostility and rejection from classmates because of their deformities, and could the cruelty of other children have pushed them toward the state of emotional imbalance that ultimately led to their criminal acts?[1]

We human beings give inordinate regard to the physical body. But if we put our self-worth in our body, we are fighting a losing battle. We can't prop it up forever. The body will hunch over and the hairs will fall out and the wrinkles will come. So where can we place our self-worth?

God Knows You

Psalm 139:1 reminds us of who we are as far as God is concerned. First, your self-esteem comes from the fact that God knows you. God is beyond the importance of the most important person you can think of, as far beyond that importance as you can possibly consider, and yet God knows *you*.

God Knows What You Do

Verse two says, "You know my sitting down and my rising up." This is a reference to the activity of life. It is an Old Testament expression that talks about the routines of life. God knew David in his active life and in his passive life. God knew what he did.

God Knows What You Think

Before you ever think your thoughts, God knows what they are. God knows your subconscious life. That's why the New Testament says that God knows what you need even before you ask.

God Knows Where You Go

In verse three we read, "You comprehend my path and my lying down, and are acquainted with all my ways." God knows all about your habits and what you need, and God knows all that's going on in your life.

God Knows What You Say

Verse four says, "For there is not a word on my tongue, but behold, O Lord, You know it altogether." Now that's kind of frightening, isn't it? It's an awesome thought that God knows everything you say.

God Knows What You Need

In verse five it says, "You have hedged me behind and before, and laid Your hand upon me." This is an Old Testament idiom that is rich in imagery. It's like saying, "You have hedged me in like a city that is under siege. You are providing and caring for me even when I don't realize it." God knows your past—He has hedged you in from behind. He knows your future—He has hedged you in before. God knows your present—He has His hand on you right now.

Stop and think about it. How important are you? God knows you. He knows what you do, what you think, where you go, what you say, what you need. When David thought about this, that God knew him out of all the billions of souls on earth, better than he was known by anyone else, he was overwhelmed. So overwhelmed that he said, "God, it's too wonderful. I just can't comprehend it."

God Is Near You

God not only knows you, He is near you. In the next six verses, the psalmist points out that there is nowhere you can go to get away from God. Often these verses are used to show that we can never get away from God—He will always find us and catch us.

But there's a positive application of this as well. This is not so much about the pursuing God but the present God. God is everywhere. He is not everything—that's pantheism. But God is everywhere.

David researches the universe as if to go through a checklist to find out if there's anyplace he could imagine where God might not be. He gives the extremes of heaven and hell and says God would be there. It may surprise you to think of God in hell. But God will be with you wherever you go, from now throughout eternity. Either as the One around whom you have wrapped your worship and love, or as the thought in your mind throughout the eternal days of the One you rejected every time you had a chance to know Him. God will be in your mind forever.

God is not only in the heights and depths, but He is in the East and the West. "If I take the wings of the morning, and dwell in the uttermost parts of the sea, even there Your hand shall lead me" (verse 9). In Hebrew, the wings of the morning are a reference to the East where the sun comes up. "The uttermost parts of the sea" is a reference to the Mediterranean Sea which was farther west than Israel.

God is in the light and in the darkness. God is near you wherever you go. You can't go to a place where God is not. God is near you. He is immediately accessible to you wherever you go.

God Made You

You are the incredible creation of the infinite God. God is involved in the conception of each of us. Verse 13, "For You formed my inward parts; You covered me in my mother's womb." These words describe reproduction in some of the most meaningful and tender verses in all of the Bible. If we read them honestly, we understand they contain the secret for an incredible sense of self-worth.

God knew you before you were born. He knows the moment when you were conceived. In every phase of development, from that moment on, He is there. The human embryo is not the result of a biological accident. God is aware of the union of the sperm and the egg and the attachment of the embryo to the uterine lining and the development of human life. God formed the inward parts and arranged the genetic structure. God knows about that human life and loves that human life from the very moment of its union.

Lewis Thomas wrote a book called *The Medusa and the Snail* about why people made such a fuss over test tube babies. Thomas said the true miracle is the common union of the sperm and egg and a process that ultimately produces a human being. "The mere existence of that cell should be one of the greatest astonishments of the earth. People ought to be walking around all day . . . calling to each other in endless wonderment, talking of nothing except that cell. . . . If anyone ever does succeed in explaining it within my lifetime, I will charter a skywriting airplane, maybe a whole fleet of them, and send them aloft to write one great exclamation point after another around the whole sky, until all my money runs out."[2]

God Protects Your Individuality

The psalmist tells us that God protects our individuality even at our birth. The phrase, "for I am fearfully and wonderfully made," means we are fearfully and *differently* made. We're all different. There have never been two human beings created alike. God has stamped us with our own special genetic code that sets us apart from every other human being on the face of the earth. Out of billions of people, God made certain that every one of us would be special. You are uniquely God's protected creation.

God Protects Your Identity

"My frame was not hidden from You," (verse 15) refers to the complete structure of the adult person. The full-grown body had actually been planned, designed, and programmed when it was not even large enough to be visible. Before you were born, the whole genetic plan of exactly what you would be as an adult was set by God. Scientists in molecular biology discovered this not too long ago. We call it DNA. In every cell of your body, there is enough information to recreate your adult person as if no other cell were necessary. And every time that cell divides in the process of your growth, all the information contained in each cell is part of the division. Someone has reasoned that if all of the instructions in the DNA of one cell were written out, it would take one thousand 600-page books to put all that information down. And God put it in a cell that no one can see without magnification. It's in every cell of your body. God did it so you would have your identity. You are unique. You are individually precious to God.

God Protects Your Importance

You are so important that all your days were written in His book before one of them came to be (see verse 16). God knew everything about you before you ever started out in life, and He has your whole life charted. He knows everything there is to know about you; you are so important to Him.

God Is Thinking of You

Your self-esteem comes from the fact that God, at this very moment, is thinking of you. In the great mind of God, He is thinking of you. Did you ever call somebody you love who was away and say to that person, "I just want you to know I'm thinking of you"? If you can't be in somebody's presence all the time, it's good to be in their thoughts. But we are in God's presence and we're in His thoughts.

The psalmist paraphrases, "If I tried to number the ways You think concerning me, I wouldn't be able to do it. Even when I'm not aware that You're thinking of me because I'm asleep, all during the time I'm sleeping, You're thinking of me. And when I wake in the morning, there You are. And Your thoughts are of me." (See verses 17–18.)

In their book, *In His Image*, Dr. Paul Brand and Philip Yancey recount how during World War II, the Germans once bombed London for fifty-seven consecutive nights, eight hours at a time. They had 1,500 bombers that came each night and they would bomb in waves of 250 bombers at a time. The only thing that stood in their way was the Royal Airforce. The flyers for the Royal Airforce were national heroes, but many of these men paid a living price for their sacrificial service. One of the types of planes they flew, the Hurricane, would burst into flame if hit. The men could eject themselves, but not before the intense heat basically erased all the features from their face.

One of these men was Peter Foster. He described what it was like to go through surgeries and prepare to re-enter public life. In the beginning, the mirror was a measuring device to see the progress the surgeons were making on his face. But as he prepared to be released from the hospital, the mirror became the reflection that showed how strangers would see him. In the hospital he had been supported by the comraderie of friends and the ministrations of the staff. On the outside, he would be a freak. "At that critical moment," said Peter Foster, "one factor alone matters—the response of your family and intimate friends."

Peter was one of the fortunate ones. His girlfriend came to the hospital and insisted they be married before he was released. She told him in no uncertain terms that she loved him, not his face. He came home on the arm of someone who loved him for who he was. There was still rejection from some people.

But Peter said, "Whenever that would happen, I would always look to my wife, and she was the one who gave me the image of myself." He said, "Even now to this day, regardless of how I feel, if I begin to feel unworthy I just look to her and she gives me a warm, loving smile that tells me I'm okay."[3]

And Psalm 139 is God's loving smile to you. You are okay. He knows you. He's near you. He made you. He's thinking of you. You're worthy because God is smiling on you today.

Notes:

1. *British Journal of Plastic Surgery,* April 2(2) 2967:204–10.

2. Thomas Lewis, *The Medusa and the Snail* (NY: Viking Press, 1979), 155–157.

3. Dr. Paul Brand and Philip Yancey, *In His Image* (Grand Rapids: Zondervan, 1984).

APPLICATION

1. Read Psalm 139:1–3.

   a. These verses show the intimate knowledge that God has of each and every one of us. In verse 1, what has God done?

   b. What does God know? (verse 2)

   c. When David says that God understands His thought "afar off," what do you think that really means?

   d. What does God comprehend? (verse 3)

e. What is God acquainted with? (verse 3)

f. What can you conclude from reading these three verses? How can that determine your self-worth?

2. Read Psalm 139:7–12.

   a. The questions in verse 7 and the lack of an answer reflect what reality?

   b. Interestingly, God is present in what two places? (verse 8)

c. Wherever we are, we are told that God's hand will do what two things for us? (verse 10)

d. We are still visible to God in what? (verse 11) For to God, the night is as bright as what?

e. Think of and describe a time when the hand of God led you and held you, even in the darkness.

3. Read Psalm 139:13–16.

   a. The God of the universe was involved in what process concerning you? (verse 13)

b. What is the psalmist's response to this amazing reality? (verse 14)

c. How can this reality give you confidence to trust God both now and in the future?

d. God was able to see each and every one of us before we were what? (verse 16)

e. Moreover, what else did God know about us before we were even formed? (verse 16)

f. In what ways has this Psalm describing God's omnipotence and sovereignty encouraged you this day?

4. Read Romans 8:13–17. What is your worth as a child of God?

DID YOU KNOW?

The complexity of the development of a baby in only nine months is a miracle that only God could orchestrate. From the initial division of cells comes a fetus whose heart develops and starts beating in as little as twenty days. And as it grows, so too do eyes, hands, a skeleton, and even an expressive face and personality. God created this process and sees it as it happens. He is the Creator of all things, especially human life. No wonder David said in Psalm 139:14 that we are, "fearfully and wonderfully made"!

HOW CAN I BE HAPPY?

Psalm 1

In this lesson we discover what leads to long-term happiness—and what doesn't.

OUTLINE

Happiness—is there anything pursued more diligently but discovered less frequently? First, there's the definition: What is true happiness? Next, there's the destination: Where is happiness found? For the psalmist, happiness is blessedness found in righteousness.

I. The Righteous Person Avoids the Downward Pull of Evil
- A. The Momentum of Influence
- B. The Momentum of Involvement
- C. The Momentum of Intensity

II. The Righteous Person Accepts the Decisive Place of Scripture
- A. Hearts Delighting in the Word of God
- B. Habits Dictated by the Word of God

III. The Ungodly Are Not So
- A. They Cannot Stand in the Time of Difficulty
- B. They Cannot Stand in the Day of Judgment
- C. They Cannot Stand in the Congregation of the Righteous

OVERVIEW

Everybody today wants to be happy. The songwriter says, "Don't worry, be happy," as if we could in some cavalier way make it happen for us. People in our culture have an incredible thirst for happiness. They will try almost anything to find it and incorporate it into their lives. But it should be evident to us that if lasting happiness could be found in having material things and being able to indulge ourselves in whatever we wanted, then most of us in America should be delirious with joy and happy beyond description. We should be producing books and poems and art that describe our unparalleled bliss.

Instead, American books and movies say to the whole world, "We've been searching for it, but we just haven't been able to find it." The search for happiness, for many, has become a journey on a dead end street.

How do we find happiness? Psalm 1 is about two roads, one that leads to God and one that leads away from God. And the way of the righteous is the way toward happiness.

The Righteous Person Avoids the Downward Pull of Evil

In order for us to understand what it means to be happy, the psalmist makes a checklist of the things people do to try to be happy. Then he says that happiness does not come from any of these things. The happy person is the one who avoids the downward pull of evil. The gravitational pull of evil is like a vortex that, once it catches us, pulls us down. Happiness is not getting caught in it.

The Momentum of Influence

We often talk about momentum—how important it is in sports, in projects, in life. But evil has momentum too. This momentum is illustrated by listing what the righteous person does not do.

"Blessed is the man who walks not in the counsel of the ungodly" (verse 1). The counsel of the ungodly is nothing less than the philosophy of the natural man who seeks to understand his existence and his control without regard to God. To be ungodly doesn't mean to be a murderer or rapist or bank robber, although it may include those things. To be ungodly means simply to live your life without God. It may not sound as bad as you thought, but in essence it's the root problem of everything.

According to the Bible, the counsel of the ungodly is the beginning place in a downward spiral. The philosophy of the ungodly is that the best way to seek key answers to life is outside of God. The innuendos and subtleties of such counsel without God begin to have an impact. That information is then translated into action. Instead of watching from a distance, a person begins to ask questions and investigate. The counsel now becomes something that has captivated him, and he wants to know more about it. Then finally he comes and sits down. That is a picture of not only being a practitioner, but settling into an embracing of this philosophy of life—a comfortable lifestyle of ungodliness.

It starts by listening to the counsel, falling into the pattern, and then settling into the lifestyle.

The Momentum of Involvement

The influence of the godless counsel translates into involvement. First you walk, then you stand, then you sit (see verse 1). Someone has described the walk as a reference to those things we decide on a daily basis. The standing is a reference to making a commitment. The sitting is a settled attitude of lifestyle. First we make little decisions that are minus God. Then we make commitments that cement those decisions. And then finally we settle into the lifestyle of a life without God.

People tell me they've come back to God after having gotten into that lifestyle. They wake up one day and say, "My goodness, twenty years ago we used to never miss church." But they made a little decision. Then out of that decision came a little commitment. Suddenly they found themselves in a lifestyle without God. That's the downward pull of evil.

The Momentum of Intensity

Three types of unrighteous people are listed in order of intensity. The first is the ungodly. That person is passive about spiritual things. He doesn't have time for spiritual things, but he doesn't mind if someone else does.

The next type is the sinner. The Hebrew word for sinner is a word which means to make a loud noise or to cause a tumult or to make trouble. It's like saying a sinner is a party animal. He's like the ungodly, not into God, but he also gets caught up in a worldly lifestyle.

The third type is the scornful. He's not influenced anymore by the people outside. He has become the influencer. He's moved from being passive about God, to practicing anti-God things, to being scornful about God. He curls his lip at God. He has fallen into the downward pull of evil.

How does a person stay away from the gravitational pull of sin? Somewhere between the counsel and the path and the seat, between walking and standing and sitting, going from ungodliness and sinning and scorning, you'll get a wake-up call from the Holy Spirit. You will feel uncomfortable. When you get that wake-up call, you've scooted over the edge; and you're about to get caught in the downdraft. When that happens, you had better move away because you are not headed toward happiness—you're headed toward misery.

The Righteous Person Accepts the Decisive Place of Scripture

The righteous person takes his delight "in the law of the Lord, and in His law he meditates day and night" (verse 2). Do you know how a lot of Christians read their Bibles? They read it to find out how far they can go before they cross the line. They don't read it to find out what God wants them to do. They read it to find out what God will let them do or what they can do without getting into a whole lot of trouble.

Hearts Delighting in the Word of God

The person who delights in the law of God is totally opposite of that. He comes to the Bible with an incredible desire in his heart to please God. That's how you delight in God's Word. If you come to God's Word with a spirit of searching for clues, you'll find little nuggets everywhere. God loves to show His children how they can please Him.

Habits Dictated by the Word of God

When you delight in the Word of God, it will determine that your habits are dictated by the Word of God. Why? Because if you're asking every day how you can please God, He will show you; and it will translate into life. Here are some clues as to what that will mean.

Your strength comes from God's Word. The righteous person is like a tree planted by streams of water. Just like a tree is nourished by the constant supply of water—without which, under the blistering sun, the tree would surely die—so the life that is rooted in the Word of God will also be established, and it will be strong.

Your stability comes from God's Word. A fruit tree that is planted by the banks of the river suggests stability. The tree is firmly rooted in the soil so that it can resist the storm. There are trees standing today that were here when this country was discovered. If you go to the right place, you can see trees that are just as magnificent and beautiful as they were in their prime. Why? They've got a tremendous root structure, and they are strong. If you've ever seen a redwood, a tree so big that you can drive your car through the middle of it, then you know what *invincible* means. That's the kind of stability God wants His people to have. And when you put your roots deep down into His Word, you will become a person of great stability.

Your spontaneity comes from God's Word. There's a phrase in verse 3 that says, "whose leaf also shall not wither." The leaf is the outward testimony of the tree. The leaf shows you what kind of a tree it is. The testimony of the Christian who is deeply rooted in God's Word will not wither. It will be a vibrant, beautiful testimony of who God is. Someone has written that all God's trees, Christians, are evergreens. Their testimony does not fall off.

There is a lot of talk about the testimony of the believer: How people we thought were great Christians withered under the pressure of temptation, under the pressure of sexuality, under the pressure of finances. But if this person withered, he wasn't rightly connected. The leaf is the outward testimony of the life that's in the person, and if you're rightly connected, your roots go down deeply into the Word of God. You are drawing energy from your time with God. You will not wither.

So if withering happens, it's not the withering that was the important thing—it was unconnectedness someplace that caused the withering to happen.

Your success comes from God's Word. The righteous person is like a tree that "brings forth its fruit in its season . . . and whatever he does shall prosper" (verse 3). Do you want to be prosperous and successful? Get your spiritual roots down deep into the Word of God. That doesn't mean you will become wealthy. The Bible has a different definition of what it means to be successful than our culture does. Someone has said that prosperity and success for the believer are like a zero. When you put a one in front of it, it becomes a ten. Add on zeros, and it can become a thousand. But unless you put the One, God Himself, at the front of it, it means nothing. Whatever God gives us—whatever success we experience—He will make it prosper because He is the One at the front of it.

The Ungodly Are Not So

Take everything that we've said about the righteous person and negate it, and that is the ungodly person. That's what the psalmist means when he says, "The ungodly are not so" (verse 4). Then he adds some more about the ungodly.

They Cannot Stand in the Time of Difficulty

The ungodly are like "the chaff which the wind drives away." It's worthless, you can't collect it, you can't use it. Get these two pictures in your mind: The tree planted by the river; the chaff which the wind blows away. Could anything more graphically describe the difference in lifestyle between a person who's firmly rooted in the Word of God and a person who is captured by the fantasies of the day and just floats around on any wind that happens to blow? The ungodly can't stand in the time of trouble because there's no stability.

They Cannot Stand in the Day of Judgment

When believers come before the Lord in judgment, they can look into the face of their Lord because they know it's okay. God has taken care of everything. The sin problem is over. Believers are accepted in the Beloved and can stand before God with confidence. But when the psalm says, "The ungodly shall not stand in the judgment" (verse 5), it means in the Hebrew that an ungodly person can only bow his head in the presence of God. He can't lift his head to look at God.

They Cannot Stand in the Congregation of the Righteous

The ungodly live today in a world where there are still many righteous people whom God calls the salt of the earth. God is not going to allow both classes of people to live together forever. Someday the ungodly are going to be separated forever from any righteous influence. That means going through eternity with the wicked and never hearing a righteous word, never witnessing a righteous act, forever and ever. I don't have to describe hell. If there were no more to it than that, that would be enough.

Charles Hadden Spurgeon wrote, "The righteous man carves his name upon the rock. The wicked man writes his remembrance in the wind. The righteous man plows furrows of earth and sows and has a harvest here which shall never be fully reaped until he enters eternity. But as for the wicked man, he plows the sea. And though there may seem to be a shining trail behind his keel, the waves pass over it and the place that knew him shall know him no more forever."[1] Happy is the one who trusts in God.

Note:

1. Charles Haddon Spurgeon, *The Treasury of David* (Hendrickson Publishers, 1988 ed).

APPLICATION

1. Read Psalm 1.

    a. Verse 1 interestingly says a man will be blessed if he doesn't do three things. What are they?

        1.

        2.

        3.

    b. All three things have in common the aspect of keeping company with what type of people?

    c. Instead, the blessed man delights in what? (verse 2) How often does he meditate on it?

d. A man who lives in such a way is like a tree planted by what? (verse 3)

e. In this metaphor, if man is the tree, what is represented by the rivers of water?

f. Because the tree's foundation is set by the water, what three good things will result?

1.

2.

3.

g. The righteous man is likened to a tree. What is the ungodly man likened to? (verse 4)

h. What will the ungodly be unable to do? (verse 5)

i. Why do you think the godly man will be able to stand in the judgment, especially in light of the metaphor of the tree?

j. The way of the righteous is marked by what? (verse 6)

k. The way of the ungodly is destined to what? (verse 6)

1. What can you actively do today to make yourself more like the blessed man described in this psalm?

2. Read Psalm 3:3.

   a. God is said to physically be what for us? (verse 3a) How can that make you happy?

   b. As well as being our glory, what does He physically do for us? (verse 3b)

   c. What does it say about God that He would be the lifter of our head? How can that relate to your perspective on happiness, including your own?

3. Read John 15:1–11.

   a. What can we do to insure that God's joy remains in us, and that our joy remains full?

   b. In John 15 Jesus explains that the evidence of joy is the bearing of fruit. What are the fruit of the Spirit? (Galatian 5:22–23)

DID YOU KNOW?

If you type in the word "happy" in Google, your search will result in more than 650 million entries. It is clearly evident that there is an obsession with happiness in our culture. But this obsession with happiness is fueled by wanting more and feeling better about oneself. This flies in the face of what Scripture teaches us. Consider Proverbs 3:13: "Happy is the man who finds wisdom, and the man who gains understanding." Talk about counter-cultural! Sadly, many who so eagerly seek happiness often are not so eager to know and practice the things of the Lord.

How Can One Book Change My Life?

Psalm 19

In this lesson we will learn two ways by which God has revealed Himself to man.

OUTLINE

Throughout history people have looked everywhere for God—in nature, in legends, in gurus, and even within themselves. God has revealed Himself in some of those ways; but without knowing what to look for, we may mistake a false god for the true God.

I. God Reveals Himself in the Skies
   A. An Undeniable Message
   B. An Unending Message
   C. A Universal Message

II. God Reveals Himself in the Scriptures
   A. It Will Restore Your Soul
   B. It Will Renew Your Mind
   C. It Will Rejoice Your Heart
   D. It Will Refocus Your Vision
   E. It Will Remain Forever
   F. It Will Refute Any Critic

OVERVIEW

The Barna research organization conducted a survey in the 1990s and reported some startling findings: only eighteen percent of those calling themselves born-again Christians read the Bible every day. More surprising was the fact that twenty-three percent of those who professed to be Christians said they never read the Bible at all.

In a day when many people believe there is no such thing as absolute truths, the Church of Jesus Christ is in danger of absorbing this belief. The only antidote to such error is to daily take in that which is absolute truth: the Word of God.

Psalm 19 declares that God has spoken to the world—He has revealed Himself to us so we can know Him. He who is Truth wants us to know what is true and so has told us in His written Word. This psalm notes three ways God has revealed Himself to us: in the skies, in the Scriptures, and in our very soul. The progression of God's revelation in the psalm goes from nature to the Word to our individual soul—from the general to the specific. In the skies, we see His glory; in the Scriptures, we see His greatness; and in our soul, we sense His grace.

God Reveals Himself in the Skies

Someone has called Psalm 8 the "night psalm" because it talks about the moon and the stars (verse 3). We could call Psalm 19 the "day psalm" because it talks about the sun in the heavens (verses 4–6). Whether in the night or in the day, God has revealed Himself to us through His creation.

An Undeniable Message (verse 1)

The message of God's revelation is undeniable: The heavens "declare" and the firmament "shows" the glory and handiwork of God. The message of God's existence and creative activity is there for everyone to see. Wherever you are on earth, look to the skies and you will see the message of the heavens.

An Unending Message (verse 2)

The message doesn't come in fits and starts—it is unending. "Day unto day . . . and night unto night" the message pours forth. Day and night swap back and forth, all day every day, revealing proof of the existence of God.

A Universal Message (verse 3)

The message of the heavens is in a language the whole world can understand. The universality of this message makes it a message to all humanity, not just to some.

The question is often raised, when discussing the gospel message, about those in distant lands who live and die without ever hearing the Gospel. What about them—are they responsible before God? The apostle Paul addressed that question in Romans 1:20 by saying, "For since the creation of the world His invisible attributes are clearly seen, being understood by the things that are made, even His eternal power and Godhead, so that they are without excuse."

While we don't understand the mystery of God's revelation in creation to the hearts of men, we do know that the heavens speak of God to the extent that man is accountable for that message. When man follows the revelation God has given, it leads to greater revelation. But too often we find people worshiping the creation rather than the Creator. They miss God and focus on what He has made instead of on Him.

God has revealed Himself in the heavens through an undeniable, unending, and universal message of truth.

GOD REVEALS HIMSELF IN THE SCRIPTURES

The psalmist now introduces how God has revealed Himself to us through the Scriptures—and He has done it six ways: law, testimonies, statutes, commandments, fear, and judgments. All these words refer to the written revelation of God in its various forms.

Through the centuries, the Bible has been scorned and attacked by its detractors. Philosophers, skeptics, emperors, professors, even some religious leaders—all have written off the Bible as being flawed and outdated. But the Bible continues to set forth the message of God's saving grace. God's revelation to man in written form continues to be the only standard of absolute truth in our world.

Reading through verses 7–9 we discover that God's revelation is characterized six ways: It is perfect, sure, right, clean, true, and righteous. Those words describe the nature of God's revelation, but they also describe the effect of God's Word on the recipient of His revelation.

In the remainder of this lesson, we will study the six ways the Word of God affects those who read it and take it to heart.

It Will Restore Your Soul (verse 7a)

Only the Bible can touch the human soul. No other book on earth has the ability to convert, or restore, the soul of man. And that means the Bible is the only book that can restore man to a place of fellowship with God. The Bible doesn't deal with our outward appearance because that is not the real, eternal part of you. The Bible deals with the inner man, the soul of man, revealing what is wrong and how it can be restored. As Hosea 6:1 says, sometimes God has to injure us before He heals us. The Word of God has the ability to diagnose, then restore, the soul of man.

It Will Renew Your Mind (verse 7b)

The Bible can make the simple (naïve) person wise by giving guidance to the inexperienced. The Bible contains practical wisdom pertaining to every area of life. I have found answers in the Bible for questions regarding family, finances, health, discipline, relationships—every spectrum of human endeavor is touched on.

It Will Rejoice Your Heart (verse 8a)

The truth of the Bible will cause your heart to rejoice, especially in times of difficulty and trouble. There are times when I get alone with God to read my Bible and listen to worship music, and my heart seems to escape the burdens of this world. I become so freshly conscious of the grace of God that I am amazed God has taken the initiative to communicate with one such as myself! And it is by reading and meditating upon the truth of God's revelation that I have that awareness. Granted, there are times when the Word of God disciplines our heart and soul, and we need that. But then there are those times when the Word rejoices the heart.

It Will Refocus Your Vision (verse 8b)

After years of taking in the ways and will of God through His revealed Word, one develops a biblical sense about life. It doesn't come from specific bits of guidance as much as from a wisdom that develops from seeing things like God sees them. We develop an awareness of the direction to go in—or not to go in. Our spiritual vision is sharpened; we gain a clearer focus on life and how to live it. The Holy Spirit uses the implanted Word of God to put a check in our spirit when we are about to make a mistake. Or we have peace and confidence when we're moving in the right direction.

We are like the person in Psalm 1: bearing fruit . . . leaves that don't wither . . . deeply rooted in truth.

It Will Remain Forever (verse 9a)

How often does the stock in a modern bookstore rotate? Constantly! But if the Lord tarries and doesn't return soon, preachers will be declaring the Word of God from the same Bible 50, 100, or more years from now. The Word of God does not change, therefore we do not need a new edition. The Bible is a timeless book. Consider those who write books in medicine, science, technology—and especially computers. These books are out of date almost before they are published, and must be constantly updated. The Bible was delivered once and for all—it is as relevant today as the day the last word was written.

It Will Refute Any Critic (verse 9b)

The Bible is self-validating and confirming—the various parts support and defend one another. It is amazing how many people throughout history have attempted to destroy or discredit the Bible by attacking its parts. But no one has been able to do it. The Bible defends itself; history and archaeology continue to support the Bible whenever a new spade of dirt is turned over.

The eighteenth-century French philosopher, a great critic of the Bible, predicted that by the time he died, the Bible would be forgotten, relegated to the dustbin of history as an ancient, antiquated book of literature. But thirty years after Voltaire's death, the World Bible Society purchased his home, installed printing presses, and began printing new copies of the Bible!

William Tyndale, the English Bible translator and distributor, was once paid a huge sum of money by an agent of the king who bought up all of Tyndale's copies to get them out of circulation. With the money, Tyndale printed up thirty times the number of Bibles he originally had. When the king demanded to know where Tyndale got the large sum needed to print so many Bibles, he was shocked that he himself had provided the money by buying up Tyndale's previous inventory.

God seems to have a sense of humor in dealing with those who try to destroy His revelation to man. A person would be foolish to try to destroy God's Bible. But even more foolish would be the person who failed to read and apply it daily to his life. The Bible is the world's most special book, "more to be desired . . . than gold . . . ; sweeter also than honey and the honeycomb" (verse 10).

There is great reward and profit in consuming and applying the truth of the Bible to one's life. It is a book with a promise. We are guaranteed a "profit" if we will only take God at His Word and live according to His statutes. My goal is not to heap guilt on those who don't read and study God's Word. We all choose what we do with our time and our life. But I do want to encourage you to let God prove Himself faithful to you by bringing reward and profit to your life through His Word. I don't know exactly how He will do that, but I know that He will because His Word promises it.

Let me share two responses to the revelation we receive from God in the skies and in the Scripture.

I live in a house situated on a mountainside in Southern California. When I go out at night and look out over the valley below, it's a moving sight. But what is incredibly more moving is to look up into the infinite skies above and know that the God who created the myriad of stars in the heavens is the same God I spoke with early that morning. Amazing! I hope I never get to the point where I am not moved by the message that comes from the heavens—that our Creator God fashioned an unfathomable universe and then reached down and touched my heart so I could know Him personally.

The same thing happens when I stand on our coastline and watch the power and immensity of the ocean at work. Or when the winds howl across our mountains and the thunder and lightning put on their display. I feel like Job who was confronted with the greatness of God in creation and came to realize He is much bigger than we can even imagine (Job 38–41). I don't need to have the revelation of God in the skies to know God in a saving way—He has provided Jesus Christ for that. But I do need to have it in order to continue growing in my love and appreciation for who God is.

I also stand in awe of God's self-revelation in the Scriptures. If God has gone so far as to promise profit and reward in life (I'm not talking about financial profit, but His overarching blessing) to those who value and consume His Word, wouldn't it make sense to begin taking it in every day? I can't imagine a more valuable enterprise to undertake, especially with all the helps that are available today for reading the Word.

There are Bibles and Bible-reading guides that are laid out for you so that all you have to do is open to today's date and read the designated portion. Giving fifteen minutes a day to that discipline will allow you to read through the whole Bible in one year. Most people could easily read the Bible in a year or less in the amount of time they spend watching television.

Another way to stay encouraged about reading the Bible is to be connected with others who are reading and studying it. Perhaps you can find an accountability partner to read with. Even better is to be involved in a small group Bible study with people who are reading the Bible regularly and getting together to discuss what they've read and how it's changing their lives. So many churches have small group programs today that are an excellent way to develop accountability and encouragement for reading the Word. All of us need accountability to do the right things in life, and that includes reading the Scriptures.

Finally, we need to be in a church where the Word of God is honored. Sadly, it isn't always easy to find such a church. If your church doesn't teach you the Bible and encourage you to become a student of Scripture yourself, I encourage you to find one that does. Better yet, be an influence in your church for the promotion of Bible reading and Bible study. Start a program, start a Bible study, start a read-the-Bible-in-a-year club. There are lots of ways for you to encourage others to benefit from the reading of the Word of God.

Lieutenant General William K. Harrison received every Army medal possible with the exception of the Medal of Honor. He was one of the most distinguished military leaders in the history of our nation. And he was also one of the most disciplined Bible readers I know of. As a young man at West Point, he began reading through the Old Testament once each year and the New Testament four times each year—and he did it for seventy years. By the time he reached age ninety, when failing eyesight forced him to stop reading, he had read the Old Testament through seventy times and the New Testament 280 times.

If a busy general, in the midst of two wars, can keep up the practice of reading God's Word daily, you and I probably can find time to do it also. May you and I follow General Harrison's, and the psalmist's, example of treasuring the revelation of God. It is the only way to make sure that the words of our mouths and the meditations of our hearts will be acceptable in God's sight, who is our Strength and our Redeemer (verse 14).

APPLICATION

1. Read Psalm 19:1–6.

   a. The heavens are more than a physical thing. What do they declare? (verse 1)

   b. What does the day do? (verse 2)

   c. What does the night reveal? (verse 2)

   d. Verse 3 tells us that all humankind can hear and understand how nature speaks of God's glory. Write down three acts of nature that speak to you of God's glory.

1.

2.

3.

e. How far has the language of nature traveled? (verse 4)

f. What is the sun described like in verse 5?

g. Verse 6 describes the cycle of the sun and its power. From what else can nothing or no one hide?

2. Read Psalm 19:7–11.

a. What is the law of the Lord? (verse 7) What does it do?

b. What is the testimony of the Lord? (verse 7) What does it do?

c. What are the statutes of the Lord? (verse 8) What do they do?

d. What is the commandment of the Lord? (verse 8) What does it do?

e. What is the fear of the Lord? (verse 9) How long does it last?

f. What are the judgments of the Lord? (verse 9)

g. Look back at the answers to questions a through f. Now write a few lines about why it is so important to implement and study the Word of God in your life.

h. God's Word is better than what precious metal? (verse 10) What is it sweeter than?

i. What are two other benefits to knowing and keeping God's Word? (verse 11)

3. Read Psalm 19:12–14.

   a. The psalmist asks God to keep him and cleanse him from what two things? (verses 12, 13)

b. The psalmist's goal is to be what? (verse 13)

c. What is the psalmist's prayer in verse 14?

4. Read Romans 1:20–21. How else does God reveal Himself to man?

DID YOU KNOW?

It is often easy to skip through portions of the Bible that are difficult to read, and to gravitate toward more gratifying portions of Scripture—like the Psalms or the four Gospels. But 2 Timothy 3:16–17 says that "All Scripture is given by inspiration of God, and is profitable for doctrine, for reproof, for correction, for instruction in righteousness, that the man of God may be complete, thoroughly equipped for every good work." And no one demonstrated this more than Jesus, who fended off Satan's temptations in the desert by quoting the often ignored book of Deuteronomy (Luke 4:1–13).

How Do I Face My Fears?

Psalm 34

In this lesson we learn to appropriate God's resources to overcome fear.

OUTLINE

Every human being on the planet shares one common predicament: not knowing the future. Fear is based in not knowing what might or will happen—fear of the unknown. Living with the God who knows everything is the first step toward living without fear.

I. Acknowledge the Reliability of Your God

II. Admit the Reality of Your Fear

III. Appropriate the Resources of Your Father

IV. Accept the Reinforcement of His Power

OVERVIEW

RIIINNNNGGGG! Your alarm clock sounds and the day begins. But instead of jumping out of bed, have you ever wanted to pull the covers over your head and hide? You dread facing all the challenges of the day. Or worse yet, if you wake up to a clock radio blaring the morning news, you know for a fact what a fearful world we live in.

But maybe your morning fears are not on the news; they're deep down in your workplace. You live in constant fear of getting caught in the down-sizing trend. Or are you working on a business deal that will determine the success or failure of your career?

Maybe your deepest fears lie at home. Is your marriage stretched to the point of snapping? Have sons or daughters drifted out of your control? Do they do drugs? Are they sexually active? I could go on and list fear after fear, but I'm sure I have already touched on some that you may know by name.

If I haven't mentioned the fear that haunts your heart, perhaps it's the illusive kind. A good friend of mine and former classmate, Don Wyrtzen, has written a little devotional book on the Psalms. Commenting on Psalm 34, he writes, "The illusive monster of fear lurks in the shadows, waiting to claw my soul to shreds. As one prone to melancholia, I see its ugly face often when I'm struggling with the emotional stress of a difficult relationship, when I'm afraid failure is just around the corner, when success seems too hard to handle, and on days when free floating anxiety is getting the best of me."

Now think about the last phrase for a moment—free floating anxiety. Perhaps your most haunting fear doesn't even have a name—that foreboding fear that something is wrong, but you don't know what. It envelopes you like a cloud. If ever you've sensed this kind of fear, you're not alone. All of us have felt that cold mist.

The psalm we are going to study speaks directly to our fears and encourages us with a wonderful promise. The truth we are about to soak up will change us if we make it a part of our lives. "The humble shall hear of it and be glad" (verse 2). In other words, if we study this psalm carefully and understand its truth, we can walk away from any fearful experience renewed in our spirit and in our heart.

In your Bible, under the title "Psalm 34," you will find a little descriptive phrase explaining the psalm's historical background: "A Psalm of David when he pretended madness before [Achish] who drove him away, and he departed."

David was a fugitive. He was fearful for his life because of King Saul's jealousy. When the young David defeated the nine foot, six inch Goliath with five smooth stones and the power of the Lord, he immediately rose to hero status in Israel with everyone except Saul. Saul wanted to kill David. He hunted him down like a wild animal. On one occasion, he amassed an army of thirty thousand men just to track him in the caves and wilderness.

David knew if he were going to escape Saul's henchmen, he would have to get creative. So, he hid in the one place Saul would never look—over the Philistine border in enemy territory. But David had forgotten that he had taken Goliath's sword as a souvenir of victory and strapped it to his belt. Crossing into enemy territory, he walked right into Goliath's hometown. David was captured within minutes and taken to their king, Achish.

David knew he was a dead man. After all, he had killed the Philistine's hero. Once again he had to use his ingenuity. So he feigned madness. First Samuel 21:13 says he drooled in his beard and scratched on the door. It was the first case of pleading insanity. He was so crazy that Achish said, "Get him out of here—I've got enough crazy people." And so David was banished from the presence of Achish, and he went down into the cave of Adullam.

While he hid in that cave, David penned Psalm 34. Does this psalm have credibility! He had been abandoned by his friends as well as his enemies. He was frustrated, discouraged, and scared to death.

I don't know what cave you're holed up in, but sooner or later we all get to the cave, don't we? We get there discouraged, wondering what's next, afraid of the future. So David wants to help us get a foothold in walking through our fears and finding God's peace with each step.

Acknowledge the Reliability of Your God

When you find yourself in the cave of fear or when that free-floating anxiety descends upon your life, the first thing you need to do is to acknowledge the reliability of your God. Say, "Lord, I know You are worthy of my complete trust." Verses 1–3 could catch you off guard if you don't understand what David is doing. These words seem better suited to a praise and worship song.

> "I will bless the Lord at all times; His praise shall continually be in my mouth.
> My soul shall make its boast in the Lord; the humble shall hear of it and be glad.
> Oh, magnify the Lord with me, and let us exalt His name together."

You may ask, "David wrote these words when he was afraid?" Yes! He wants us to understand that when we as believers in God face our fears, we must start with the realization that God is sovereign—He's in charge. He's in total control and He is worthy of our praise. Nothing that happens to us catches Him by surprise.

David dealt with his fear by offering praise and worship to God. He demonstrated his faith in the Lord by looking immediately into His face. He shows us that we need to express our love, appreciation, praise, and exultation to the One who is in charge. Three times he says it in three different phrases: "I will praise the Lord no matter what happens. I will constantly speak of His glories and grace. I will boast of His kindness to me."

When I feel afraid, I'm prone to pull the blanket over my head and hope it goes away. Or I nurse my fears. The adversary of our souls loves to get our attention focused on ourselves and not on the resources of our God.

What will happen when you praise and worship God? Your praise makes God big in your heart and mind. Soon, your problem falls into perspective. When I worship God, sometimes even with the tears coming down my face, my spirit is renewed as I praise God. My problem doesn't go away, but all of a sudden I see it in relation to the One who is in charge of everything.

I like that last little phrase, "I will boast of His kindness to me." It's interesting what we boast about, isn't it? At the last party you went to, what did you boast about? Put the spotlight on the Lord and focus on Him. When we get together with friends, let's just brag on Jesus. A friend of mine says that every time something good happens, we should have a "Yea, God!" party. David agrees! He shows us that one of the great therapies for fear is to have "Yea, God!" parties. So many good things are happening in our lives as individuals, in our families and churches, that we ought to boast on the Lord all the time.

Admit the Reality of Your Fear

Most of us know that God is trustworthy. But the next step could cause us to trip a bit. In the beginning of Psalm 34, we have to admit to the reality of our fears. Read verses 4 and 5: "I sought the Lord, and He heard me, and delivered me from all my fears. They looked to Him and were radiant, and their faces were not ashamed."

David, the poet, personifies his fears. The verse literally reads, "I will never put a veil over the face of my fears, I will never try to hide them." David explains in poetic form that part of the process of dealing with fear is the willingness to acknowledge and admit the fear is there.

I don't like to acknowledge my fears to anyone. It's kind of stupid, but I don't even like to tell God. Then I think, "Good night, Jeremiah, He knows about them already. But I still have a hard time saying, "God, I'm afraid," or, "God, I'm weak." We ought to acknowledge our fears before God.

Why? Only the fearful, the weak, and the helpless ever get the power of God in their lives. Did you know that? Look down in the next verses. Verse 6 says, "This poor man cried out." He didn't say "This strong man cried out . . . this man who has it all together cried out." David said "This poor man . . ." He recognized his need for God.

When we try to live our lives in our own strength, we ultimately fail. And if we don't fail, we fall very short of God's purposes for us. When we operate in the flesh, three things are always true: (1) We will always lack the power of the Spirit, and we'll suffer from fatigue; (2) we will always lack the vision of the Spirit, so we'll suffer from frustration; and (3) we will always lack the sustaining ministry of the Spirit, so we'll suffer from failure.

Do these consequences sound familiar? You will always suffer these results when you tackle life in your own strength. But when tragedy strikes—an illness, financial hardship, rebellious children—you turn to God. When you feel helpless, inadequate, and weak, the Spirit of God gives you strength. All of a sudden you realize something dynamic is going on that you have never experienced before. It's not your power; it's God's power. The apostle Paul admits that if it takes weakness to get God's power in his life, he's better off weak than strong. When you are weak, then you are strong (2 Corinthians 12:8–10).

Appropriate the Resources of Your Father

David testified, "This poor man cried out, and the Lord heard him, and saved him out of all his troubles." C. S. Lewis once wrote, "Down through the ages whenever men had a need of courage they would cry out 'Billy Budd, help me' and nothing happened. But for 1900 years, whenever men have needed courage and have cried out, 'Lord Jesus, help me,' something always happened."

I love the Hebrew definition of the word "trouble." The word literally translates, "hang-ups." It means to be inhibited, tied up and restricted. When we lay hold of Christ, we are freed from our "hang-ups." David reviews this principle later in verses 15 and 17. "The eyes of the Lord are on the righteous, and His ears are open to their cry. . . . and the Lord hears, and delivers them out of all their troubles."

Sound too simple? It is! Yet when I've counseled with many Christians in deep trouble, I've asked them, "Have you talked to the Lord about this?" They looked at me with a blank stare. "You mean tell Him?" Yes. When you acknowledge the reliability of the One who is in charge of your life and then admit your fear, you have to appropriate the power that He has promised to give you. You have to tell it to Jesus.

Accept the Reinforcement of His Power

When you tell it to Jesus, you now have His great resources coming to your aid. "The angel of the Lord encamps all around those who fear Him, and delivers them" (verse 7). Focus on that for just a moment. The phrase "angel of the Lord" appears in the Psalms three times, but you will never find it in the New Testament. This phrase is an Old Testament theophany which is an appearance or manifestation of God on Earth. A theophany is the Old Testament picture of Christ. In other words, the "angel of the Lord" is the Christ of the New Testament operating in the Old Testament. You don't need the angel of the Lord in the New Testament because you have Christ.

Christ, the Lord Jehovah, encamps around those who fear Him, and He delivers them. Jesus is close to you during the most fearful moments of your life. It doesn't say He removes the fearful situation, but it promises that He will be encamped around you. The word "encamp" literally means to fortify you, build a hedge around you, and protect you in the midst of every fearful experience.

Have you ever gone through a difficult time and testified, "I never have felt so close to God like I did during this trial." That was the presence of God fortifying you—strengthening you in the hard times.

Psalm 34:18 says, "The Lord is near to those who have a broken heart, and saves such as have a contrite spirit." Do you have a broken heart? Are you filled with fear? Let me comfort you with something about the Lord, my friend. He is near you. Worship Him, tell Him your fears, receive His strength, and trust Him to filter everything that touches you through His fingers of love.

APPLICATION

1. Read Psalm 34:1–3.

   a. What is the overall tone of these three verses? What is David doing?

   b. What can we take away from the fact that in a time of great fear, the first thing David does is magnify the Lord?

   c. When should the praise of God be in our mouths and hearts? (verse 1)

   d. What will its effect be upon the humble? (verse 2) Why do you think this is so?

e. Verse 3 is an invitation to magnify God in what way?

2. Read Psalm 34:4–7.

   a. When David sought the Lord, what two things did He do in turn? (verse 4)

   b. What did the Lord do for the poor man? (verse 6)

   c. What will the angel of the Lord do for those who fear God? (verse 7)

d. What actions and realities in verses 4–7 can help you to not be afraid?

3. Read Psalm 34:8–10.

   a. Those who "taste and see" will discover what about the Lord? (verse 8)

   b. The man who trusts in God is what? (verse 8)

   c. Instead of fearing man, what are we to fear? (verse 9)

   d. What is the positive result of fearing God? (verse 9)

e. Verse 10 reiterates the main theme of these three verses. What is that theme?

4. Read Psalm 34:17–18.

a. What do the righteous do when they are fearful? (verse 17)

b. What happens when they do this? (verse 17)

c. Where is God when we have a broken heart? (verse 18)

d. What will God do for those who have a contrite spirit? (verse 18)

e. The next time you are fearful, what are you going to do? Why?

5. Read 1 John 4:4–18. What is the promise found in verse 18?

DID YOU KNOW?

Although we live in a modern world full of convenience, we are still a very fearful people. There are doctors, psychiatrists, and clinics who are devoted solely to treating the anxieties and fears that people face. And we have created names for phobias about every possible thing. Apiphobia is the fear of bees. Logizomechanophobia is the fear of computers. We even have a word for the fear of beards–pogonophobia! But whatever our fears and anxieties may be, God's Word tells us to give all these things to the Lord and to claim the truth of Proverbs 3:5–6: "Trust in the Lord with all your heart, and lean not on your own understanding; in all your ways acknowledge Him, and He shall direct your paths."

How Can I Help My Family?

Psalm 127

In this lesson we discover four biblical principles that lead to fruitful families.

OUTLINE

No one enters into family life intending to be regretful and discouraged twenty years later—but it happens. Busyness, conflict, and out-of-sync priorities can take their toll. Following God's principles for family life is the only safe way to proceed.

I. Place God at the Head of Your Home

II. Put Parenting at the Top of Your Priority List

III. Protect Your Family From Destructive Influences

IV. Praise God Openly for Your Children

OVERVIEW

The few verses in Psalm 126 give an overarching principle that affects the family. It says, "Those who sow in tears shall reap in joy. He who continually goes forth weeping, bearing seed for sowing, shall doubtless come again with rejoicing, bringing his sheaves with him" (verses 5–6). It's a reminder that the principle of sowing and reaping is at work in our families as well as the rest of life. What happens in our families has a lot to do with what input we give.

Sadly, many of us try every modern approach to family life, only to discover that while it may fix one part of the family, it ends up messing up the rest of the family. God has a better idea. In fact, the family is one of God's greatest ideas for us in this universe.

In the beginning of the Bible, right after the story of creation, God looked at man and said, "It is not good that man should be alone" (Genesis 2:18). He brought a woman to him. And family began. If God had the idea about family, doesn't it make sense that He has something to say about how we can make the family work?

Not only in the Psalms but through all of the Bible, God has incredible truths to help us build families that will bring honor and glory to His name.

Place God at the Head of Your Home

The first principle is that if you are going to be successful in building a family, you have to place God at the head of your home. Psalm 127:1 says, "Unless the Lord builds the house, they labor in vain who build it." This is the most important truth in building a home. It's saying if God doesn't build it, it isn't going to work. There is only one builder in the home, and that builder is God. God, who had the idea of the home, is the One who wants to be at the head of the home. Until God is at the center of your home, all your attempts at making family life what you want it to be will be attempts in frustration. Unless you let Him build the home, you're going to do it in vain.

How many people do you know who thought that if they got all the things their family wanted, their family would be a strong family? How many kids do you know who have so many things, but they have no family? There is no one there for them. That's not

God's plan. God's plan is to be the head of your home. You may be thinking: There's no way I'm going to install halos on my kids. They wouldn't look right and they wouldn't fit. I don't want Bible verses like mantras around the house and little Christian plaques up on the walls.

But that's not what it means to have God at the head of the home. When I was growing up, I knew that God was central in my home. But it wasn't because we read the Bible after dinner every night. It wasn't because my parents were in institutional ministry or that my parents preached at me. It was that God was important to my parents. Everything we were involved in, God was there as part of the picture. Most of the time He was the centerpiece. But wherever He was, He was a part of the family. As I grew up, I couldn't escape that.

We communicate our values where they really are. You can't fake it with kids. You can try to make them believe that God is important, but it's not going to get through unless God really is important to you. The best thing we could do before we install God at the head of the home is to install Him at the head of our life. Then we can ask Him to live that out little by little in our families.

Put Parenting at the Top of Your Priority List

"Unless the Lord builds the house, they labor in vain who build it" (Psalm 127:1). God declares what I've always suspected—that being a parent is labor. It's hard work. That's a simple concept, but it's losing its value in our culture today. Parenting is being pushed over the edge while moms and dads pursue their professional goals and purposes in life. God is saying that He has given us the plan, but we are the laborers. We have to put in the time and make parenting important or it won't work.

Wherever I go to speak, one of the first questions I get asked is—can you tell us a little about your priorities? Priorities are important because they govern your life. And it's one thing to talk about your priorities, it's another to put them into perspective and live by them. Some time ago I took time with the Lord and tried to get a clear understanding of what my priorities were. They don't necessarily have to be your priorities, but most of us are going to fall into the pattern of the following priorities.

First, I am a person, and I had better take care of my personal relationship with God. God is number one. In fact, He says He must be number one. He is a jealous God and He doesn't want anybody to come between the two of us. He's number one in my life, and so I need to cultivate that relationship. I have to spend time with God.

Second, I'm a partner, and I've got a wife. A wonderfully, wonderfully good wife. She's number two. God is first. Donna's second.

Third, I'm a parent, and I've got children. Four of them. They're the most important thing in my life outside of God and Donna. And every day of my life I have to fight to preserve that priority.

Years ago this priority was tested when I was invited to speak at a convention to 450 women. The convention was in March, far beyond the time when my son's basketball season was over. I didn't schedule anything during the basketball season or the football season if I could help it. But the basketball team kept winning. They got in the playoffs and they kept winning. I was supposed to be at the convention from Thursday through Saturday. But our guys won all their games and were supposed to play for the city championship on Saturday morning. So I had my secretary call and say I couldn't be there on Saturday.

At the convention hotel lobby, I met a woman who said, "Let me tell you right up front, we're so glad you're not staying for Saturday." I thought—this lady hasn't even heard me speak yet and she's already made up her mind. Then she said something I will never forget. She said, "We are all wives of executive husbands. It's just so incredibly encouraging to see somebody in a position of leadership make a decision in favor of their family."

I was speaking on Friday when a woman got up and ran out of the building with tears running down her face. Later, I asked the director of the conference if I had said anything to offend that woman. She went to find out, and she told me the woman had heard about how I was leaving the conference early to go to the game on Saturday. Her daughter was playing for the state championship in Denver on Saturday, and she got so convicted she left the meeting, packed her clothes, got on a plane, and went home.

We should put our children in a place where once in a while they understand that they're important. Make parenting a priority. Even if we don't do anything else with our life, making parenting a priority is a full-time task.

Protect Your Family From Destructive Influences

The second part of verse 1 changes the metaphor a bit. It says, "Unless the Lord guards the city, the watchman stays awake in vain. It is vain for you to rise up early, to sit up late." We've seen the family get built like you build a house. Now we have a picture of a city that is a protection for its people. While it is important for us to come to God and let Him be the builder of our families, when our families are built, we have to come back to God and ask Him to help us be the watchmen over our families. It's a picture of a parent looking out over his family and protecting it and watching out for it. And if there's ever been a time when we need to do that, it's now.

Once again, we are in partnership with God. Just as there's one builder and two laborers and we're working together on the same project, there's One who is the watchman, but we're to be watchmen with Him.

There is a common problem in our culture today: children left to themselves to grow up with no protecting influences around them, and with no one seeming to care. Sometimes it's necessary for both parents to work in order to make ends meet. But if they're doing it to maintain a higher standard of living, then that's a foolish decision. They're giving up their children for more toys.

How do you protect your children in partnership with God? By praying. Our kids are in intense battles, and they need to know that Mom and Dad are standing with them and praying with them.

As your kids grow older, the control over their lives gradually shifts from you to your children. Ultimately, as parents, we'll say good-bye to them. What's incredible is that one way you can stay in touch with them is through prayer. I meet God at the throne of grace every day and touch a loved one 3,000 miles away from me. I can talk to God about them, and God hears.

Praise God Openly for Your Children

Psalm 127:3–5 says, "Behold, children are a heritage from the Lord, the fruit of the womb is a reward. Like arrows in the hand of a warrior, so are the children of one's youth. Happy is the man who has his quiver full of them; they shall not be ashamed, but shall speak with their enemies in the gate." It's the best thing that Solomon could say in his language about parenting. Be positive about being a family. Realize that God gave you your children as a gift. Children are God's blessing to us.

Solomon says they are like arrows. What does an arrow do? It goes to a place you can't go and accomplishes a purpose you can't accomplish. Isn't it incredible to see how God raises up our children and thrusts them out? Whatever good your children are doing out there, there's a part of you that's doing it too because they're an arrow that's gone out from your bow to do good for God.

This passage gives a picture of what can happen when you and your children get older. In Solomon's day, all major disputes were decided at the gate of the city. If we raise good children, our children will be there to help us out and speak for us and stand with us when we need them.

A seaplane careened into the sea off the Alaskan coast and capsized. After determining that everyone was alive, including his twelve-year-old son, Dr. Phil Littleford suggested they pray, which the two other men quickly endorsed. No safety equipment could be found on board. Fortunately they all had waders which they inflated. They began to swim for shore, but the riptide countered every stroke. The two other men both made shore, one just catching the tip of land as the tides pulled them out towards the sea. The two men last saw Phil and Mark as a disappearing dot on the horizon, swept arm in arm out to sea. The Coast Guard reported they probably lasted no more than an hour in the freezing waters. Hypothermia chilled the body functions and they went to sleep. Mark, with the smaller body mass, fell asleep in his father's arms. Phil could have made the shoreline too, but that would have meant abandoning his son.

The writer asks, What father wouldn't be willing to die for his son? Most of us would be willing to put ourselves in harm's way to protect our children. But if we are willing to go so far as to die for our children, why is it so hard for many of us to live for them? Tragedy is no less painful if it's by the sudden stroke of drowning than if it's the protracted hurt of a disenfranchised child who has been swept away in the world and has lost all hope of ever recovering. God has put us, as parents in this world, to stand in harm's way for our kids.

APPLICATION

1. Read Genesis 18:19.

   a. God makes Himself known to us so that we can command whom?

   b. What are we to command them in?

   c. What does keeping the way of the Lord involve doing?

   d. This picture of the family in Genesis still applies today. What action can you take to better lead your family in the way of the Lord?

2. Read Deuteronomy 6:6–9.

   a. Where should the commands of God be written? (verse 6)

   b. What should we do with these commands? (verse 7a)

c. Verse 7b says that we are to talk of the things of the Lord even in the midst of four different actions that happen throughout the day. List them below.

1.

2.

3.

4.

d. Give your interpretation of what you believe the commands of verses 8–9 mean, and how you can carry them out in your own home.

3. Read Psalm 127.

a. Verse 1 declares that the work we do is in vain unless what?

b. Verse 2 lists three other things that are all done in vain unless the Lord is involved.

   Name them.

   1.

   2.

   3.

c. Have you ever been involved in those activities listed without the Lord? How did it work out for you? How did you feel?

d. According to this passage, what are children? (verse 3) What is the fruit of the womb?

e. What are children likened to in verse 4? Why do you think that is so?

f. The man who has such children is described to be what? (verse 5)

g. What can you do to make sure the Lord is in the work of your family so that it is all not done in vain?

DID YOU KNOW?

Today's culture seems intent on destroying the family. The destruction of marriage and the home is coming from all angles, from the prevalence of divorce to the redefinition of marriage itself. But God still holds marriage and the family to be of the utmost importance. Consider Genesis 2:23-24: "This is now bone of my bones and flesh of my flesh; she shall be called Woman, because she was taken out of Man. Therefore a man shall leave his father and mother and be joined to his wife, and they shall become one flesh." This is God's plan. And it is reiterated even more strongly in the New Testament that husband and wife are not to divorce (1 Corinthians 7:10–11). May we all heed God's Word and follow His commands.

Why Do Good Things Happen to Bad People?

Psalm 73

In this lesson we learn why it's important to view life from God's perspective.

OUTLINE

Sometimes the child of God wonders if it's worth it to be faithful. After all, ungodly people seem to ignore God and float through life without a care. But when we see life from God's perspective, we discover that the ungodly have a rude awakening coming.

I. Inner Conflict

II. Outward Contradiction
- A. Bothered by Their Prosperity
- B. Bothered by Their Pride
- C. Bothered by Their Profanity
- D. Bothered by Their Popularity

III. Upward Confidence
- A. Resist the Urge to Voice Doubts
- B. Return to the Presence of God
- C. Review the Rest of the Story
- D. Reevaluate Your Own Life
- E. Reassure Your Heart of God's Love and Goodness
- F. Reestablish Your Faith in God
- G. Resolve to Stay Near God

OVERVIEW

One of the delights of being a parent or a Sunday school teacher or a backyard Bible club leader is getting to hear the questions children ask. The younger they are, it seems, the more honest and uninhibited their questions are—even when they're addressing God in their prayers. Little children are not afraid to ask anything.

Unfortunately, the older we get—and especially the more mature we get in the Lord—the more we lose our willingness to ask hard questions. We think that if we're truly spiritual we won't have any hard questions to ask. But the truth is, the older we get, and the longer we live in this world, the more questions we have about "how things work." For instance, why do bad things happen to good people and good things happen to bad people?

A psalmist named Asaph had questions like that as he looked around his Old Testament world. And he put them in the form of a psalm that we will study in this lesson: Psalm 73.

Inner Conflict

Asaph began with the inner conflict he was experiencing as he observed what, to him, looked peculiar and inconsistent with God's promises and character: the wicked were prospering (verse 3). God had promised to bless those who loved and obeyed Him, but it appeared that the ungodly were also being blessed.

Not only were the ungodly being blessed, Asaph, who was trying to be a faithful Jew and walk in fellowship with God, wasn't being blessed. His life was filled with confusing circumstances and painful concerns. There was a resentment growing in him over why God wasn't blessing him the way He appeared to be blessing the ungodly around him (those who lived their lives oblivious to God and His requirements). He was close to stumbling in his faith over this issue.

Outward Contradiction

The source of Asaph's conflict is the contradiction he saw between those who didn't even try to do good, sailing through life without a minute's trouble, and those who try to serve the Lord, living lives filled with trouble and need. He had an inner conflict based on an outward contradiction. There were four realities that seemed contradictory to Asaph.

Bothered by Their Prosperity

First, the ungodly were prosperous (verses 3–5). Wrapped up in the word "prosperity" is the idea of peace and complacency. The ungodly didn't seem to have a care in the world—no pain, no struggles, no problems. They didn't even die in pain. They lived in ease and died in ease. Asaph couldn't figure this out.

Bothered by Their Pride

Verses 6–7 reveal that not only did they enjoy lives of ease, they were proud of it. It didn't bother them that they were proud and violent people—but it bothered Asaph. And it really bothered him that it didn't seem to bother God! It was one thing for them to prosper, but it was another thing for them to boast about it and get away with it.

Bothered by Their Profanity

The third thing that bothered Asaph was the profanity of the ungodly (verses 8–9). They mocked the God of heaven in their boastings. They tried to make those who trusted in God look like fools for their faith. "We don't trust God," they would say, "and look at us. We're better off than you!"

Bothered by Their Popularity

The straw that broke Asaph's back is this last one: The ungodly were the most popular people around (verses 10–11). People envied their prosperity, their pride, and their profanity. People crowded around them, believing that God doesn't really know what's going on.

I remember when a member of the mafia was put on trial and how the news was full of pictures of him coming to the trial in a limousine dressed in expensive suits. Many people admired him and were angry that he was being prosecuted. It's easy to get caught up in following the lifestyles of the ungodly. We read magazines and watch TV shows dedicated to following their every move. There is little to commend them as objects of admiration, yet people adore them. And Asaph said, "It doesn't make sense."

In verses 13–14 he confessed that maybe his efforts to live a godly life had been in vain; maybe it had all been for nothing. After all, if the ungodly can live a blessed life without trying to please God, what's the point in trying?

I doubt if there is a serious Christian alive today who hasn't entertained some similar thoughts in his lifetime. What if . . . ?

What if they're right and I'm wrong? What if I'm missing out on the fun in life by not trying to get everything I can while I can get it? Maybe there's nothing at all after we die. Maybe I'll look ridiculous in the end for believing something that really wasn't true.

Those are hard questions—but they are honest ones. And they deserve honest answers, which is what Asaph discovered as he pondered his situation.

Upward Confidence

Asaph's inner conflict developed into an upward confidence in God as he began to think logically through what he observed in the world. By going through the seven steps Asaph went through, we can address our own doubts when we have them.

Resist the Urge to Voice Doubts

First, Asaph decided to be careful about who he voiced his doubts to—specifically, to people who wouldn't understand (verse 15). Voicing your legitimate doubts to some people might destroy their faith. Asaph realized that to be totally honest and open in a public venue might plant seeds of doubt in God's children, so he decided to be circumspect in what he said and to whom.

Asaph might have had doubts and frustration, but he still had wisdom. He knew it would be unwise to harm anyone else's faith with his own doubts (understandable though his questions may be).

Return to the Presence of God

In verse 17 we find Asaph returning to the source of all truth: "the sanctuary of God." Only when he got into the presence of God did he understand the truth about the ungodly: "Surely You set them in slippery places; You cast them down to destruction. Oh, how they are brought to desolation, as in a moment! They are utterly consumed with terrors" (verses 18–19). Asaph submitted his rational thinking—the kind of thinking with which contradictions in logic are easily spotted—to the spiritual reasoning of God.

In the temple, Asaph allowed God to become part of the equation. His perspective was broadened to include God's perspective—and everything changed. Instead of seeing just a small portion of the situation, Asaph began to see what God sees. It's impossible to see things from God's point of view without getting close to God. Instead of judging life on the basis of externalities—money, success, popularity—Asaph began to look at life from a spiritual point of view.

There is a temptation when faced with spiritual questions to do just the opposite of what we should do: We're tempted to withdraw from God in frustration and discouragement. Instead, we should do what Asaph did: Enter into the presence of God to get His perspective.

Review the Rest of the Story

Asaph's third step was to review the rest of the story. Just as the famous radio journalist Paul Harvey revealed "the rest of the story" to help us better understand what happened in a given situation, so Asaph began to understand the rest of the story of the ungodly. All he saw was their public prosperity and popularity. He didn't know anything about the rest of their lives. But if the ungodly in his day were anything like the ungodly in our day, there was a lot of their story that the public wouldn't see. And that part of the story is not always one we would want for ourselves.

Asaph saw that the ungodly were "utterly consumed with terrors" in spite of their seeming peace and happy-go-lucky attitude. There were things that not even money could provide, and in those cases they had nowhere to turn for help. Prosperity could not save them from judgment they would face before the God they had mocked all their lives. We could make a long list of the celebrities in our culture whose lives have ended in tragedy, whose money and fame were not enough to rescue them from terror and torment at the end of their lives.

About halfway between Los Angeles and San Francisco is the William Randolph Hearst castle, built decades ago by one of America's wealthiest men. But Mr. Hearst had a rule in his house: Death was never to be mentioned. He was afraid to go to sleep at night so tormented was he by the fear of death—the fear of going to sleep and never waking up. Asaph might have looked at Mr. Hearst and his castle and wondered why he had been blessed with such abundance. But then he would have gone home and enjoyed a good night's sleep, secure in his eternal life, something Mr. Hearst could not do.

I remember as a child having a fear of the dark when my grandparents' town would have blackout drills during the days of the Cold War. The sirens would wail and the lights would go out and I would be terrified. But since coming to Christ and understanding my eternal security in Him, there has not been a night I have gone to sleep afraid of the dark or of death. I wouldn't trade that security for all the castles in the world—nor would Asaph.

Reevaluate Your Own Life

In contemplating the anxiety he had entered over the status of the ungodly, Asaph confessed, "Thus my heart was grieved, and I was vexed in my mind. I was so foolish and ignorant; I was like a beast before You" (verses 21–22). Asaph was wise enough to admit the error of his ways. It is that kind of honest confession that will keep us from making the same mistakes again and again in life. In modern language, Asaph might have said, "Man, I feel really dumb for getting all exercised over that issue."

All of us feel like we've been "had" at times. We wonder how we could have been so gullible. The problem is we don't see it until after it's happened. Hindsight is always 20/20, isn't it? But we can learn. We can learn to get into the presence of God at the very first sign of something challenging our peace and contentment. Stopping such challenges at the outset will save us much unnecessary anxiety. It is easy to pamper ourselves, to justify our discontent, to rationalize our frustration. Whenever we find ourselves doing that, we need to get in the presence of God and ask for His perspective on the situation.

Reassure Your Heart of God's Love and Goodness

Verse 23 begins with a watershed word: "Nevertheless . . . ." When we see that word, we know that Asaph is starting down the other side of the huge mountain of discontent he has been climbing. "Nevertheless"—meaning, "In spite of the fact that I got sucked into frustration and discontent—I am continually with You; You hold me by my right hand. You will guide me with Your counsel, and afterward receive me to glory" (verses 23–24).

Even though Asaph had been questioning God, God had never let go of Asaph's hand. God was with him the whole time, leading him to the future glory planned for him. Asaph had a startling revelation: In spite of what appears to be inequities in this world, they do not affect his relationship with God. Asaph is not loved any less because the ungodly appear to be getting away unpunished. God has not started favoring the ungodly over the godly. Asaph is reassured of God's continual love for him.

Reestablish Your Faith in God

Asaph is moving in a straight line back to reaffirming his relationship with God: "Whom have I in heaven but You? And there is none upon earth that I desire besides You. My flesh and my heart fail; but God is the strength of my heart and my portion forever" (verses 25–26). He confesses that having God is having the most important possession of all.

We can look around at this world and think it would be nice to drive the fanciest car and live in a castle and travel on a private jet as some do. While no one would say it's wrong to have or do those things, it is a fact that none of those things will get you to heaven. Jesus asked what good it is for a person to gain the whole world yet lose his soul in the end (Matthew 16:26). God has given us plenty to enjoy on this earth and also the ability to enjoy, but He never intended for any part of the creation to replace Him as the focus of our life. If we spend our days being envious of those who have everything except trouble, we will find ourselves in an endless cycle of discontent.

Asaph was nearly destroyed in that cycle until he woke up and realized he had the most important thing of all: God Himself.

Resolve to Stay Near God

The reason Asaph realized that staying near to God was the best thing he could do was that "those who are far from [God] shall perish" (verse 27). That's not complicated, is it? Would you rather have everything this world has, care nothing about God, and perish, or have God's plenteous provision, be close to God, and be saved? That is not a difficult choice.

If you compare all the things Asaph said about the ungodly at the beginning of this psalm with everything he said about them at the end, you see they are completely reversed. What made the difference? Asaph's getting into the presence of God is what completely changed his perspective (verse 17). He began to see the wicked and ungodly for what they are: mockers of God who will ultimately perish without Him. Their prosperity, pride, profanity, and popularity will not be enough to save them in the final analysis. But the godly, those who are mocked and ridiculed by the ungodly, are going to be led through this world by the hand of God and straight into eternity.

The apostle James put it well in his letter when he wrote, "Draw near to God and He will draw near to you" (James 4:8). That's what Asaph discovered—or confirmed—after he drew near to God in the sanctuary of God. He found that God was still near him, that God had never left him regardless of how it had appeared.

Learn from Asaph. Don't be led astray by the seeming immunity of the ungodly to trouble, or your seeming fill of it. If you are God's, He has you by the hand. Draw near to Him and you will see everything just as He does.

APPLICATION

1. Read Psalm 73:1–3.

   a. Verse 1 acknowledges that God is good to those who are what?

   b. What almost happens to the psalmist in verse 2?

   c. Why did he almost stumble and fall? (verse 3)

   d. Can you share in his frustration in the things you see and experience today?

2. Read Psalm 73:4–9.

   a. What do the wicked appear to be? (verse 4)

b. What do the wicked seem to avoid? (verse 5)

c. What is their necklace? (verse 6) Their garment?

d. What do they possess materially? (verse 7)

e. What do they speak about? (verse 8) How do they speak it?

f. Interpret the image of the tongue and the mouth in verse 9. What do you think it means to set it "against the heavens" and that it "walks through the earth"?

3. Read Psalm 73:10–17.

   a. In this passage, what two things characterize the ungodly? (verse 12)

b. What does the psalmist believe he has done in vain in light of this? (verse 13)

c. What has he been experiencing while the wicked have prospered? (verse 14)

d. When all these things came together, what was it like for him? (verse 16)

e. What did it take for him to gain an appropriate and eternal perspective on all these things? (verse 17)

4. Read Psalm 73:18–20.

   a. What has God really done with the wicked and the ungodly? (verse 18)

b. How quickly are they destroyed? (verse 19) What consumes them?

c. What will happen when God awakes His wrath on them? (verse 20)

5. Read Psalm 73:27–28.
   a. What will happen to the deserters of God? (verse 27)

   b. What is it good for the godly to do, especially when the wicked are prospering? (verse 28)

   c. Where has the psalmist put his trust? (verse 28) So that he may do what?

d. How can you reconcile your own struggles as the wicked prosper around you?

6. Read 1 Timothy 6:6–12. How do these verses help you view your life from God's perspective?

DID YOU KNOW?

The Bible itself holds conclusive evidence that God will judge the wicked and will not let them linger indefinitely without judgment. Just consider the book of Genesis. Not once, but twice did God levy His wrath upon the wickedness set before Him. God famously flooded the entire planet to rid it of the ungodly, sparing only Noah and his family (Genesis 6:5–7). And later on, God utterly destroyed Sodom and Gomorrah for the same abhorrent behavior (Genesis 19:24–25). But in His mercy, God spared Lot (Genesis 19:29) just as He had spared Noah. Our God of wrath and judgment is also a God of mercy and grace.

How Can I Be Truly Forgiven?

Psalms 32 & 51

In this lesson we learn how to be forgiven for any sin.

OUTLINE

Human nature is to keep quiet about sin. But when a major figure in the Old Testament sinned, he learned there is one person who does not overlook or excuse it: God. He also learned that, while God does not overlook sin, He also is willing to forgive sin if we ask.

I. Conviction

II. Confrontation

III. Confession
- A. Genuine
- B. God-Centered

IV. Cleansing

V. Consequences

OVERVIEW

Katherine Anne Power was an accomplice in a Boston bank robbery in 1970 in which a Boston policeman, the father of nine children, was killed. She was not the robber, nor the shooter of the policeman, but the driver of the getaway car. She avoided arrest and for the next twenty-three years hid her past. She deliberately lost touch with her parents, changed her name, and tried to fade into anonymity. But at age forty-four, suffering from chronic depression, she could no longer live with her guilt and efforts to conceal her past.

U.S. News and World Report quoted Power's therapist as saying, "Power realized that her emotional difficulties would never end until she came clean and gave herself up as a fugitive." Though she had avoided law enforcement officers for twenty-three years, she had not been able to escape her own guilt and shame over the crime in which she participated. After turning herself in, Power is quoted as saying that ten years in prison would be better than the prison she had lived in for twenty-three years.

David, the king of Israel, was racked with guilt for a year before confessing his own sin. He tried to cover up what he had done, but came clean when he was confronted. We find David's story in 2 Samuel 11–12, his confession and cleansing in Psalms 32 and 51.

David's life took a dramatic turn from being a man after God's own heart to an adulterer and murderer who tried to cover up his sin for almost a year. David took Bathsheba for himself and had her husband, Uriah, one of his trusted soldiers, killed. He had even brought Uriah home from the battlefield to sleep with his wife so it would appear Bathsheba's pregnancy was due to her husband. But Uriah refused to enjoy the pleasure of his wife's company while his fellow soldiers were still in the field, camping out instead near the palace of David, his commander. Uriah was an honorable man whom David had killed by telling Joab, the commander, to put him in the fiercest part of the next battle so he would be killed. David's adultery led to murder, and he tried to cover up these sins for a year. At the end of that time, Psalms 32 and 51 were written.

During that year, mourning for Uriah was completed and David took Bathsheba for his wife. David was suffering with guilt (Psalm 32), but did not come forward. "But the thing that David had done displeased the Lord" (2 Samuel 11:27). God knew what David had done.

David's experience is a case study in what happens when sin is not confessed and how we should deal with the issue of guilt.

Conviction

Like Katherine Power, David experienced extreme anguish during the year he kept quiet about his sins (Psalm 32:3–4). He talks about groaning all day long and the loss of his vitality. His guilt impacted him physically. He would probably have agreed with Katherine Power's description of her own symptoms: "Waves and waves of depression came one right after the other, and I could hardly stand them."

After a year (Bathsheba's baby had been born; 2 Samuel 11:27) God sent someone to David to help him get rid of his sin and guilt.

Confrontation

The Lord sent Nathan, a prophet, to confront David (2 Samuel 12:1–15). What would you have done if the Lord had told you to go and confront the king about his sin? Nathan did it indirectly by telling David a story about a wealthy man who abused a poor man in hopes of David condemning the actions of the wealthy man.

Here's the story Nathan told: There were two men in a city, one rich and one poor. The rich man had many flocks and herds, but the poor man had nothing but a single lamb that his family loved. When the rich man needed to prepare a meal for a visitor, instead of taking a lamb from his own flock, he took the lamb of the poor man, killed it, and prepared it for his visitor's meal.

Here's what Nathan was communicating: David was the rich man, Uriah was the poor man, and Bathsheba was the lamb. When David heard Nathan's parable, he was enraged. He swore that this wealthy man would die for his unconscionable act against the defenseless poor man: "And he shall restore fourfold for the lamb, because he did this thing and because he had no pity" (2 Samuel 12:6). In other words, the meaning of the story went right over David's head in terms of its application to himself. He got the point, but missed the application.

Because David did not see himself as the guilty "rich man," Nathan had to make the point: "You are the man!" (verse 7) Nathan was putting his neck on the line by accusing the king, but he figured it was better to anger the king than to disobey God.

Lots of people would prefer to go through life without ever hearing a discussion about sin. Even many Christians would prefer it if they never heard about sin in the church. But let me remind you that David was confronted about his sin not because Nathan was nosy, but because God was concerned. God wanted David to face up to what he had done and restore his conscience—for his own good! And I dare say that when Nathan said to David, "You are the man!" that David was relieved, glad to finally have his web of deceit uncovered and broken; glad that he could finally be free of his guilt.

I have learned in my own life and in counseling others that there is usually no change without confrontation. If we reject the "confronter" we will not grow. But if we will accept the confrontation God orchestrates, we will change and become better for it. David could have had Nathan killed and remained in denial and deceit. Instead, he accepted his guilt and confessed his sin.

Confession

The superscription to Psalm 51 (the part of the psalm written just before verse one, which is part of the biblical text) tells us the occasion of the psalm's writing: "A Psalm of David when Nathan the prophet went to him, after he had gone in to Bathsheba." Charles Spurgeon suggests that this was likely the first thing David had written since committing his double sins of adultery and murder. He probably wouldn't have been able to write anything, given the condition of his heart that had become a harbor for sin. But after being confronted by Nathan, after agreeing with Nathan's accusation, David took up his pen and wrote of his confession and cleansing by God.

There are two characteristics of the words David penned: They are genuine, and they are God-centered.

Genuine

Not all confession is genuine. The story is told of a man who wrote a check to the IRS to confess that he had misrepresented his income the previous year on his tax form. He wrote, "I haven't been able to sleep because of what I did. I'm enclosing a check for $150. If I still can't sleep, I'll send the rest of what I owe." That's not genuine confession.

Many people will confess only up to the point that they have agreed with what has already been discovered. They won't confess to everything—only to the extent their sins have been found out. That is not genuine confession, either.

The way we know David's confession was genuine was by what he said. In Psalm 32 he calls his sin transgression (which means rebellion) and iniquity (which means perversion, distortion, acting unjustly, dealing crookedly) (verses 1–2). David did not try to sugarcoat what he did. He used words to describe his sin that, in Hebrew, are very graphic. He said to God, "I acknowledged my sin to You, and my iniquity I have not hidden" (verse 5). The only kind of heart God honors is a broken and contrite one (Psalm 51:17), and that is what David had.

The human tendency is to try to make sin look as attractive as we can, to try to put the best face possible on what we've done wrong. But the word "confess" means to say the same thing as. If we are confessing to God, it means to say the same thing about our sin as God says. Therefore, to truly confess, we can't put a happy face on sin. We have to call it what it is, call it the way God sees it. And that is what David did. His confession was genuine.

God-Centered

The second characteristic of David's confession was that it was God-centered. He prayed, "Against You, You only, have I sinned, and done this evil in Your sight . . ." (Psalm 51:4a). This is not to be insensitive to the others harmed by his sin. Uriah was dead, Joab was involved unwittingly, Bathsheba had been shamed, and an illegitimate child had been brought into the world. But David recognized that all sin was ultimately against God.

When a person recognizes that sin is, first and foremost, a sin against the love and grace of God, that person has taken the first step back toward reconciliation with God. Sometimes people would rather confess their sin to God than to another person because they think they can just say a quick little prayer and be done with it. But if we understood who God really is and what it means to offend His holiness and majesty, we would not feel that way. The way we worship God is a good indicator of who we believe He is.

David's confession was genuine because it was God-centered. He confessed what he had done and against whom.

Cleansing

David understood his record in heaven had a stain on it, and he wanted that stain removed. He asked God to remove the stain next to his name: "Purge me with hyssop, and I shall be clean; wash me, and I shall be whiter than snow . . . . and blot out all my iniquities" (Psalm 51:7, 9). Like striking a word out of a document with a large black marker, David wanted the record of his sin to be blotted out of heaven's archives.

But it was not only the record of heaven that David wanted to be pure. He wanted to be pure himself. He wanted to be cleansed from his sin (verse 2); he wanted to be washed "whiter than snow" (verse 7); he wanted to have a clean heart and a new, steadfast spirit within him (verse 10).

One of the most insightful phrases in Psalm 51 is in verse 7: "Purge me with hyssop." Hyssop was a plant used in purification rites. When a person came in contact with a dead body, they had to be purged (cleansed) with hyssop. David saw himself as the cause of Uriah's death and so knew he needed to be purged with hyssop. He says he will be "clean" if purged, a word in Hebrew that means "un-sinned." He wants God to "un-sin" him, to make him as if he had not sinned. That's not great English, but it's great spiritual language.

It is no wonder that David says, in Psalm 32:2, "Blessed is the man" who does what he has done; the man "whose transgression is forgiven, whose sin is covered" (verse 1). David had sinned, had been confronted, had confessed, and was now clean. He was on the other side of the events that happened a year earlier. And he describes himself as "blessed." He wrote Psalm 32 to proclaim the blessedness of cleansing from sin and to warn others about the folly of concealing sin (verses 9–11). Anyone who has ever been forgiven for his sin knows what David is talking about—as do those who have refused to confess and be cleansed.

Psalm 86:5 says, "For You, Lord, are good, and ready to forgive, and abundant in mercy to all those who call upon You." And Psalm 103:11–12 says, "For as the heavens are high above the earth, so great is His mercy toward those who fear Him; as far as the east is from the west, so far has He removed our transgressions from us."

God is ready to forgive all who call upon Him, ready to remove their sin as far from them as the east is from the west, as far as the heavens are above the earth.

Consequences

There is always a postscript to sin, a postscript called consequences. Forgiveness does not erase history or the consequences of our acts. God forgives but He doesn't automatically wipe out the results of our actions and choices.

Katherine Power, in the article about her, wondered aloud about all those who had suffered because of her actions: the children who lost their father, her own family who lost their daughter, her own husband whose wife was now in jail, or her own son who lost his mother. Even when we recognize our choices were wrong, we can't undo the harm that has been done.

When David declared to Nathan that the wealthy man who stole the lamb would pay four-fold, he was being prophetic. David paid a heavy price for his sins of murder and adultery.

The child Bathsheba conceived and bore died. David lost credibility as a father to his existing children. His son, Amnon, raped his own half-sister, David's daughter Tamar. David failed to bring justice to bear on Amnon so Absalom, David's son and Tamar's brother, took matters into his own hands and murdered Amnon. Finally, Absalom got into a power struggle with his father David and tried to wrest the kingdom from him. He rebelled against David and took half the people of Judah with him, forcing David to flee for his safety. But then Joab killed Absalom for his rebellion against David.

David's life took a tragic turn after his sins: a dead infant, a raped daughter, and two dead sons. Would any of these things have happened anyway if he hadn't sinned? Certainly the infant would not have been brought forth to die. The rest, we do not know. But it is easy to see how David's sins destroyed his credibility in his family.

The point is that we reap what we sow (Galatians 6:7). Our actions always have reactions. God forgives, but the consequences of our sins are not automatically taken away.

Two concluding lessons: First, it is impossible to get away with sin (Numbers 32:23). God sees everything and either now or in the future will bring all unconfessed sins to light—yours and mine. Second, God forgives. If you have sinned (and you have, Romans 3:23), the Bible promises God's forgiveness if you will seek it. I hope you will.

APPLICATION

1. Read Psalm 32.

   a. A man is considered to be blessed when God does what for him? (verse 1)

   b. In contrast, what are the effects of holding on to sin? (verse 3)

   c. What important step does the psalmist make in the road to forgiveness? (verse 5a)

   d. What does God in His mercy do in turn? (verse 5b)

e. In verse 7a, what is God described as? Why do you think the psalmist chose that term specifically?

f. What are two things that David says God will do? (verse 7)

g. Recall and describe a time when God gave you a song of deliverance.

h. What do the wicked have to look forward to? (verse 10) What about those who trust in God?

i. What should be the response of those who love the Lord and have experienced His forgiveness? (verse 11)

2. Read Psalm 51.

   a. Once again, what important act does David do to initiate the cycle of forgiveness? (verse 3)

   b. When we sin, what are we really sinning against? (verse 4)

   c. List all the verbs that are used to describe all the actions God takes when He forgives us. (verses 7–9)

d. David specifically asks God to do four things in verses 10–11. Name them.

   1.

   2.

   3.

   4.

e. When God restores David, what will David do in turn out of joy? (verse 13)

f. What are the sacrifices of God? (verse 17) What will He not do with these things?

3. Read Psalm 86:3–5.

   a. As a precursor to forgiveness, what has David been doing? (verses 3 and 4)

b. Is it possible to experience the forgiveness of God without true repentance and confession? Why or why not?

c. What is God ready to do when we cry out to Him? (verse 5) What will He abundantly give?

4. Read Ephesians 1:3–7 and Romans 6:1–14. What do these verses say about the forgiveness of sin?

DID YOU KNOW?

There are innumerable verses in Scripture that deal with forgiveness, and it only makes sense—we are fallen and fallible creatures and are always in need of forgiveness for violating God's perfect law. Leviticus chapter 4 describes all that had to be done to make a sin offering. It was a detailed, precise, and bloody procedure. In light of that, we should be all the more grateful for Christ and His sacrifice for us. Because of Christ, we can share in the promise of Acts 5:31—"Him God has exalted to His right hand to be Prince and Savior, to give repentance to Israel and forgiveness of sins."

So Why Should I Be Thankful?

Psalm 92

In this lesson we learn why there are many reasons to be grateful to God.

OUTLINE

On any given day, we can look around and find things for which we don't feel particularly grateful. But on the same day, if we will, we can find more reasons *to* be thankful than not. Gratitude is a discipline developed by intentionally looking up, around, and within.

I. A Thankful Heart Causes Us to Look Upward

II. A Thankful Heart Causes Us to Look Around

A. Relationships

B. Circumstances

III. A Thankful Heart Causes Us to Look Within

OVERVIEW

In *The Haunted Man*, Charles Dickens tells of a chemist troubled with unhappy memories. A phantom offers the haunted man the opportunity to have his memory destroyed. He accepts the offer and not only loses his memory, but gains the power to strip others of their memories as well. The gift was a big disappointment. The man's misery was so great that he asked the phantom to come back. The tale concludes with the man's grateful and earnest prayer: "Lord, keep my memory green." Keep my memory green. Memory is a word which is both bitter and sweet. It is a strong argument for the soul and for life and for life hereafter.

Someone said memory is "The well-stored library of the mind." Memory makes the joys of childhood live again. Memory in the night makes past days appear all over again. Memory restores the blessedness that once we knew when we saw the Lord. And I love this definition best: "Memory is the angel with the backward look." Memory is the key to gratitude.

Amnesia literally means "without any memory." We might wish we had amnesia about some things, but it would be very difficult for us to be grateful people if we could not remember what God has done for us. Psalm 92:1-2 says, "It is good to give thanks to the Lord, and to sing praises to Your name, O Most High; to declare Your lovingkindness in the morning, and Your faithfulness every night."

It's good to give thanks and sing praises because "You, Lord, have made me glad through Your work; I will triumph in the works of Your hands" (verse 4).

Verse 5: "O Lord, how great are Your works! Your thoughts are very deep." In verse 8 he says, "But You, Lord, are on high forevermore."

A Thankful Heart Causes Us to Look Upward

Giving thanks causes us to look upward. Thanksgiving is what we offer God for what He has given us. Psalm 107:21–22 says, "Oh, that men would give thanks to the Lord for His goodness, and for His wonderful works to the children of men! Let them sacrifice the sacrifices of thanksgiving, and declare His works with rejoicing."

The apostle Paul went through many difficult things in his lifetime, yet he remained grateful and focused on God. He wrote to the Ephesians, "giving thanks always for all things to God" (Ephesians 5:20). He wrote to the Colossians, "And whatever you do in word or deed, do all in the name of the Lord Jesus, giving thanks to God the Father through Him" (Colossians 3:17). To the Thessalonians he said, "We give thanks to God always for you" (1 Thessalonians 1:2). To young Timothy he wrote, "I thank Christ Jesus our Lord who has enabled me" (1 Timothy 1:12). He wrote to Philemon, "I thank my God, making mention of you always in my prayers" (Philemon 1:4).

I keep a prayer journal in which I have a section for thanksgiving. At first I thought I would just write what I am thankful for, but I decided that wasn't a good habit. So I began to write out "Thank You, God, for . . ." There are whole pages in that journal filled with thank-you's to God.

A Thankful Heart Causes Us to Look Around

Giving thanks is good also because it causes us to look around.

Relationships

In addition to his relationship with God, Paul had relationships with people. He couldn't close a letter without naming all the people with him and all the people at the letter's destination. He talks about them with fondness, mentions their names, and usually says something about them. He is always giving thanks to God for people. In 1 Timothy 2:1, he says, "Therefore I exhort first of all that supplications, prayers, intercessions, and giving of thanks be made for all men." Paul says we're to give thanks to God for our friends and for our loved ones. He does that often in his epistles. In Acts 28:15 he says, "And from there, when the brethren heard about us, they came to meet us as far as Appii Forum and Three Inns. When Paul saw them, he thanked God and took courage." Every time Paul was next to somebody whom God sent to minister to him, he was filled with gratitude. In Romans 6:17 he writes, "But God be thanked that though you were slaves of sin, yet you obeyed from the heart." All of his letters seem to be salted with gratitude for relationships.

I don't think God ever intended for us to be loners. "The Lone Ranger" is a good story, but it's not a good lifestyle. Whenever people tell me what God is doing, they speak of relationships. They've discovered that growth in the spiritual realm is a lot easier when you grow together with another person who helps and encourages you. I don't think you can undersell the importance of friendship. If you have someone you're close to, somebody who ministers to you, puts an arm around you on occasion, cries and laughs with you, the relationship is a very, very important thing for which to give thanks.

In the Bible Belt, they have revival meetings. (We don't have them much on the West Coast.) I went to preach at one for four nights. On Tuesday night after I finished preaching, a young woman told me an experience she had.

She said, "I'm embarrassed to tell you this, Pastor Jeremiah, but Friday I was on my way to take my life. I was so discouraged and felt so useless and worthless. I turned the radio on and I heard this guy teaching the life of David. He was talking about Saul's suicide."

She continued, "As I drove down the highway, I heard this man say, 'Some of you may be thinking of doing what Saul did, but don't you do it. It's not what God wants for you.' It shocked me. It was almost like the voice on the radio was talking right to me. I pulled my car off the road, and all I could do was cry.

"I called a friend and she came and got me. She took me to her house, and I stayed with her and her husband all weekend. They wouldn't let me leave because they were afraid of what I might do. On Monday she was invited to a revival meeting in Greensboro, North Carolina. When the friend told her a man named David Jeremiah was speaking at the revival, I said, 'That's the man I heard talking to me on the radio Friday! What's he doing in Greensboro?'"

As I talked with this young woman, I could tell she was deeply troubled and was going through real struggles. She came to the services every night that week. On Thursday night she came forward and gave her life to Christ. I'm not exaggerating when I say I've never seen a person so visibly transformed by an encounter with the almighty God. Her face, her countenance, her whole bearing changed. Jesus Christ had come to live within her, and I knew she was a new creation.

God had sent a friend who came and got her at the point of her crisis, put her arm around her, and brought her into her home. Then that friend brought the desperate young woman to hear a message that would help her accept the Lord. When she thanks

God for her salvation, she will be very grateful that He sent a friend to help her through a difficult time.

Relationships are vital to our growth and maturity as Christians. When you look around, you can't help but be thankful for friendships.

Circumstances

We need to be thankful for circumstances, too. I once read a silly little cartoon around Thanksgiving that said, "I won't say this has been a trying year, but this is the first Thanksgiving we had a turkey volunteer." That's really a trying year. Some of you have been through a year like that.

Please look back at Psalm 92:2 and notice it says to "declare Your lovingkindness in the morning, and Your faithfulness every night." When I wake up in the morning, I feel the sense of God's presence in my life. I'm grateful for the night of rest (if indeed it has been such a night) and for being refreshed for the new day.

The Hebrew word that is translated "lovingkindness" is a rich word that describes the goodness and graciousness of God. In the morning, the psalmist is overwhelmed with God's lovingkindness. But at night, it's a different word. It's His faithfulness. Haven't we all looked back on a day and seen many places where we could have walked astray if God had not been good to us? We thank Him that He has been faithful to us. In Psalm 119:62, the psalmist even plans to arise and give thanks at midnight.

The Bible tells us to give thanks all of our lives, day in and day out, regardless of the circumstances. I read a poem once that suggested we even take a grateful approach to housework. A sink full of dirty dishes can make us grateful that we have food to eat. Dirty laundry can make us appreciate nice clothes to wear. Unmade beds can remind us to thank God for a good night's sleep. A dirty bathroom can even make us grateful we have modern conveniences.

Everything that is a difficulty in our eyes is usually, if we look behind it, the evidence of something good God has done for us. When you're expressing gratitude, look up at God, then at the people around you and the circumstances God has brought into your life.

A Thankful Heart Causes Us to Look Within

Giving thanks causes us to look within ourselves, also. When you review this year, what do you see that God has done in your life?

How has He helped you grow? Has He strengthened you? Can you look back and say, "It hasn't been a great year for me, but I have learned a lot about God during this year"?

One writer expressed his gratitude this way:

Lord, thank You for the gift of good health.
Thank You for eyes that see the beauty of Your creation.
For ears that receive the world of sound surrounding us.
Thank You for the special stimulation of taste and touch.
For hands to work with and legs to walk with.
For a mind that is curious and creative and competent.
For memories of past pleasures.
For heartaches that force me to rearrange my priorities.
For broken dreams and lingering affliction that humbles me.
For the courage to tell the truth when it really hurts.
For the determination to finish a demanding task.
For a sense of humor that brought healing and hope.

And for the sheer delight of knowing and walking with You for another year.

When I look inward, I see the traces of God's hand in my life. I'm not the same man I was last year. Though I'm not what I want to be and not what I ought to be, thank God I'm not what I was.

First we look up. Then we look around. Then we look in.

Louis Smedes wrote an interesting little book called *A Pretty Good Person*. He talks about courage and grit and all of this sort of thing; but right up front, interestingly enough, he talks about the fact that a pretty good person is a person with gratitude.

In the book he tells how one cold December morning his wife found him nearly dead on the kitchen floor of their apartment. An ambulance rushed him to the hospital where they diagnosed that his lungs had numerous blood clots. He survived the twenty-to-one odds against him, and one night he woke feeling extremely grateful.

He says,

I was flying outside of myself. High. Held in weightless lightness as if my earthly existence needed no ground to rest in but was hung in space with only love to keep it aloft. I was so grateful. It was then that I learned that gratitude is the best feeling I would ever feel in all of my life. It was the ultimate joy of living. It was better than winning the lottery. Better than watching your daughter graduate from college. Better and deeper than any other feeling. It is, perhaps, the genesis of all other really good feelings in the human repertoire. I am sure that nothing in life can ever match the feeling of being fully, totally, completely grateful.[1]

To feel thankful, you don't have to promote it or force it. What you have to do is get alone with your Bible. Read a psalm. Then do three things: Look upward, look around, and look inside.

Note:

1. Louis B. Smedes, *A Pretty Good Person* (New York: Harper Collins, 1991).

APPLICATION

1. Psalm 92:1–4.

   a. What two things is it good to do? (verse 1)

   b. What does the psalmist do in the morning? (verse 2) At night?

   c. Verse 3 shows that the psalmist is giving his praise through music. Why is singing praises to God such a powerful and important thing to do?

   d. How has the Lord made the psalmist glad? (verse 4) What will he do in turn?

2. Read Psalm 92:5–11.

   a. What reality do the foolish not understand? (verse 5-6)

   b. Verse 7 gives us an interesting twist on why the wicked are allowed to prosper. Why does God let them flourish?

   c. For how long is God ruler of all things? (verse 8)

   d. Two things will happen to the enemies of God. What are they? (verse 9)

      1.

      2.

e. In contrast, what two things will God do for those who love Him? (verse 10)

1.

2.

3. Read Psalm 92:12–15.

a. What will the righteous flourish like? (verse 12) What do you think the psalmist is trying to convey by using such an image?

b. What happens if you are planted in the house of the Lord? (verse 13) Explain what you think that means.

c. Those who are rooted in God will still do what in their later years? (verse 14) List some of those fruits that you hope to still be bearing as you continue to serve God.

d. What three things does the psalmist declare? (verse 15)

1.

2.

3.

4. After reading through this Psalm, what are you thankful for? What promise of God has encouraged your heart this day?

5. Read Psalm 95:1-7. What are we called to do?

6. Read Psalm 18:46–49. According to these verses, why should we thank God?

DID YOU KNOW?

Being thankful is an essential part of being a follower of Christ. If you are not thankful, you need to examine your heart and make sure you are truly glorifying God and serving Him. Romans 1:21 describes people who knew God but "did not glorify Him as God, nor were thankful." What happened to such people? They became "futile in their thoughts, and their foolish hearts were darkened." In fact, God gave them over to their sins and "vile passions." So be thankful for what God has done in your life. Thank Him not only for salvation, but for every breath and moment He gives you on earth.

WHAT CAN I DO WHEN TROUBLE OVERWHELMS ME?

Psalm 27

In this lesson we discover how to respond to troubles and trials.

OUTLINE

Many Christians mistakenly believe the Christian life is supposed to be trouble free. It is not a question of "if" we will experience trials and tribulations in this life, but "when." Instead of taking away trouble, God provides instructions for how to overcome it.

I. David's Principles
- A. Express Your Faith
- B. Extend Your Faith
- C. Experience Your Faith
- D. Enjoy Your Faith

II. David's Prayer
- A. True Prayer Responds to God's Call
- B. True Prayer Relies on God's Provision
- C. True Prayer Resigns to God's Will
- D. True Prayer Remains Calm When God Delays

OVERVIEW

David spoke about trouble in the famous 27th Psalm. When he wrote this, he was probably running from Saul in fear. Some have suggested that he may have written it when Absalom, his son, committed treason against his own father. Whenever it was written, we do know the 27th Psalm is the personal testimony of a man who is in trouble. Despite the many moods reflected in this psalm, it is quite evident the psalmist knew what to do when trouble visited his life. We shouldn't be surprised if, on occasion, it visits our lives, too.

This deeply spiritual psalm is easily divided into two sections. Verses 1–6 give the psalmist's testimony of how he dealt with fear and trouble. Then, almost as an illustration for us, verses 7–14 are a prayer David prayed when he was in trouble.

David's Principles

Express Your Faith

David said in verse 1, "The Lord is my light and my salvation; whom shall I fear? The Lord is the strength of my life; of whom shall I be afraid?" We know David is in trouble, and fear is knocking on his door. The rest of the psalm speaks of his enemies and trouble. Yet, here he is expressing his faith out loud and aggressively. He is saying what he knows even though his feelings don't match what he's expressing.

When the disciples were in a boat with Jesus and He was asleep, storms came and waves began to rise. The disciples were terrified, and finally one of them cried out, "Teacher, do You not care if we perish?" Jesus raised His arms, and said, "Peace be still," and the storm subsided. Then he turned and rebuked His disciples, saying, "Why are you afraid? Have you no faith?" (Mark 4:38–40)

He was reminding them that He was with them. We can't have a blind kind of simple faith that's not objectively attached to anything and get through fear. Jesus was saying that as a believer in Him, you don't go through trouble alone. In the midst of his trouble, David can say, "The Lord is my light and my salvation, and I know that I don't have to be afraid" (Psalm 27:1).

I find that when trouble visits my life, I often need to speak out loud what I'm not really too sure about in my feelings. I say, "Lord,

I don't really feel like this is true, but I know You are my strength. You are my salvation." By expressing your faith during the time of trouble, you take the first step toward healing and wholeness.

Extend Your Faith

I want you to notice that secondly, David moved from expressing his faith to extending his faith. I once read a secular management book that suggested writing catastrophe reports. In the midst of your trouble, you sit down with a yellow pad of paper, imagine the worst result you could have from the trouble you're experiencing, and write it in detail. When you read it aloud, you realize this problem probably won't get that bad, and you start feeling better.

David has written a catastrophe report in this psalm. He has extended his fear to its logical boundaries. Notice he says in verse 3 that he won't fear if an army camps against him. He'll be confident even if war rises against him.

Sometimes we spend so much time talking about what's wrong in our lives, we don't take enough time to express our faith and say, "Lord, even if this bad situation got ten times worse, You would still be there for me. I have confidence in this. You are the God of the extremes in my life." Express your faith, and then extend your faith.

Experience Your Faith

In verses 4 and 5, David talks about experiencing his faith. He says, "One thing I have desired of the Lord, that will I seek: that I may dwell in the house of the Lord all the days of my life, to behold the beauty of the Lord, and to inquire in His temple. For in the time of trouble He shall hide me in His pavilion; in the secret place of His tabernacle He shall hide me; He shall set me high upon a rock."

This is a wonderful, rich verse. David has now whittled his life down to one thing. He says, "One thing I have desired of the Lord, that will I seek." It reminds me of Philippians 3:13–14 where Paul says, "One thing I do, forgetting those things which are behind and reaching forward to those things which are ahead, I press toward the goal for the prize of the upward call of God in Christ Jesus."

David says the one thing he'll do when trouble comes is center his thoughts on God. He'll go into the temple, the sanctuary, where God is. He'll meditate on the beauty of God and spend time with God's people.

When problems come to many people, the first thing they do is quit coming to church where they would have been confronted with the Word of God. David speaks about it openly and says, "In the midst of my trouble, I come to the Lord's house." At this time, the temple wasn't even built yet, so David went to a tent. The temple, for David, was the place where the Ark of the Covenant was kept. It was where the presence of God was expressed. So what David said was essentially, "When my enemies encamp around me, and I feel trouble pressing in upon me, the one thing I won't ever do is let it get between God and me." He's like a military man who has found a refuge, a fortress.

If you allow trouble to come between you and God, it will move you away from Him. But if you refuse to let trouble separate you from God, it will stay on the outside and be a force that pushes you toward God. It all depends on where you let the trouble come into your life.

Enjoy Your Faith

Not only do we need to experience our faith, but verse 6 says we need to enjoy our faith. "And now my head shall be lifted up above my enemies all around me; therefore I will offer sacrifices of joy in His tabernacle; I will sing, yes, I will sing praises to the Lord."

Praise is not just worship; praise is also warfare. When we feel least like worshiping God, that's when we need to worship Him most.

Have you ever seen people with so much trouble their heads are down? Have you felt that way? You face a confrontation and it goes wrong. You walk away from there with your head down. Very graphic, isn't it? The Bible says when you face trouble and you worship, that worship becomes the lifter of your head. You could walk into church with the burdens of the world on you; and when you get caught up in the worship of the Lord, it's almost like God just lifts your head right up.

Worship makes God big in your heart. Is God big? Yes. He can't get any bigger than He is. I mean, God is God. He's the ultimate bigness. But worship magnifies God; it puts awareness of who God is into your heart so you begin to sense and appreciate the greatness of Almighty God. When you see His greatness and you put your trouble in that picture, everything changes. When you measure your trouble against others, you might be depressed; but when you measure your trouble against the greatness and magnificence of God, that's a great thing. No wonder your head gets lifted.

Those are the principles David tells us in verses 1–6 of Psalm 27. Then in verses 7–14, he prays.

David's Prayer

True Prayer Responds to God's Call

When we study this prayer, we understand how to pray when trouble comes. In verses 7–8, David says, "Hear, O Lord, when I cry with my voice! Have mercy also upon me, and answer me. When You said, 'Seek My face,' my heart said to You, 'Your face, Lord, I will seek.'" True prayer in time of trouble is really a response to God calling us. Isn't it interesting that even when trouble overwhelms us, some of us aren't prone to take the first step toward God? We're stubborn. The Bible calls us "stiff-necked." When trouble comes, we have an incredible urge to try to work it out ourselves. Sometimes God's the last option on a long list of options.

In the midst of his trouble, he heard God say, "Seek My face, David." David obeyed. In every difficult situation, there's always a time in the midst of it when the voice of God speaks to us and says to us, "Seek My face." When this happens to you, respond. True prayer in time of trouble is really a response to God.

True Prayer Relies on God's Provision

True prayer in time of trouble relies on God's provision. David says in verses 9 and 10, "Do not hide Your face from me; do not turn Your servant away in anger; You have been my help; do not leave me nor forsake me, O God of my salvation. When my father and my mother forsake me, then the Lord will take care of me." David realizes how dependent he is on God, so dependent that he said, "God, even if it were true that my father and my mother could forsake me, I know that You would take care of me." David's father and mother never forsook him. He's using it as an illustration. Even if his mom and dad kicked him out and disowned him, he knows God would never do that. When David wrote this psalm, he may not have known about the breakup of the family in our day, but his words can comfort those whose parents have rejected them because of their faith in God. Even if your mother and father forsake you, God will be there to provide for you. He is your Father, your Heavenly Father.

True Prayer Resigns to God's Will

David's prayer is a prayer of humble submission to God's will. In verse 11, he says, "Teach me Your way, O Lord, and lead me in a smooth path, because of my enemies." He's not trying to sort out his trouble himself, nor, "Lord, I've figured out my way, now You bless it." He's saying, "Here's a blank sheet of paper. I have no idea how to get out of this trouble. You fill in the page. I'll sign the bottom of it, Lord."

Perhaps because of some experiences I've been having in my own life, I almost came out of my chair when I understood what David said in verse 13: "I would have lost heart, unless I had believed that I would see the goodness of the Lord in the land of the living." This is not about seeing the goodness of the Lord in the sky by and by, but about seeing it in the land of the living, here and now. It's as if David is saying, "I would have fainted. I would have given up. I would have lost my will to go on, if I had not believed I would see Your hand of goodness in the here and now."

I don't have to debate with you about the goodness of the Lord in the land of the living. We expect that as God's people, but sometimes we don't see it because we don't look for it. I've been keeping track of the goodness of God in the land of my living. I keep a little journal in which I write things God does. My list is growing. When I'm in trouble and my faith gets down to a flickering flame, I open up my journal and read my list that shows the goodness of God in the land of my living. It has been a great encouragement to me. If we don't recognize the goodness of God, our prayers will be anemic.

True Prayer Remains Calm When God Delays

God isn't on our time schedule. We need to remain calm when God delays. Sometimes when we pray, "Lord, help," He doesn't do it right away. Verse 14 says, "Wait on the Lord; be of good courage, and He shall strengthen your heart; wait, I say, on the Lord!"

When trouble comes, express, extend, experience, and enjoy your faith. When you pray in times of trouble, respond to God, rely on Him, resign to His will, and remain calm until His help arrives. All of these principles are available to you just like they were to David. You can write your own psalm, and God will hear you.

APPLICATION

1. Read Psalm 27:1–3.

   a. The Lord is what two things? (verse 1a) Because of this, what is David's attitude?

   b. Verse 1b reiterates the very same thought. Why is he unafraid?

   c. What were the intentions of the wicked? (verse 2) What happened instead?

   d. David was so confident in the Lord that he didn't even fear what? (verse 3)

e. Do you share in David's confidence in God? Why or why not?

2. Read Psalm 27:4–6.

a. David's desires are pure. Where does he want to dwell? (verse 4)

b. What does he want to behold? (verse 4)

c. Where does he want to inquire?

d. David knows that in troubled times, God will do three things for him. What are they? (verse 5)

1.

2.

3.

e. From what will he be lifted up? (verse 6a)

f. Because of all these things that God will do, what will David do in turn? (verse 6b)

3. Read Psalm 27:7–14.

a. What are we to do in times of trouble? (verses 7-8)

b. What three things does David ask God not to do? (verse 9) Is God faithful to that request?

c. The Lord promises to take care of us even when who will forsake us? (verse 10)

d. David's prayer in verse 11 can be ours as well. What is it?

e. What would have happened if David had not seen God's goodness? (verse 13)

f. This psalm ends with powerful and practical advice that we all should heed. What is it? (verse 14)

4. Read Psalm 42:5 and remember that our hope is in our faithful God.

DID YOU KNOW?

Think of all the times that God delivered His people out of trouble. He raised up Moses to deliver the Israelites from Pharaoh, and even parted the Red Sea to ensure their safety (Exodus 14:30). And in the life of David alone, God helped him defeat not only a giant (1 Samuel 17:50), but also allowed him to become king and even bring the ark of God back to Jerusalem (2 Samuel 6:12). If God saw fit not only to save but even use a stutterer and a shepherd to bring Him glory, imagine what He will do for you if you only trust Him!

ADDITIONAL RESOURCES
BY DR. DAVID JEREMIAH

Where to Go in the New Testament When . . .

We've all experienced challenging moments that leave us asking questions. Whether it's not knowing how to witness to a friend, or it's learning how to fight temptation, we've all been in need of answers and solutions. This guide is arranged topically, containing multiple Scriptures that address more than 50 different areas of life, like "Prophecy, End Times," and "Lead Someone to Jesus." Small enough to take on the go, this New Testament guide is useful for personal study or to witness to others and contains completely new information not found in *Where to Go in the Bible When . . .* the first guide in this two-volume series.

Answers to Questions About Heaven

Heaven is mentioned often in Scripture—more than 500 times—making it clear that God wants us to envision and anticipate the place He has prepared for us. *Answers to Questions About Heaven* will whet your appetite for the place Jesus is preparing for us and will leave you offering afresh the last prayer of the Bible: "Even so, come, Lord Jesus!"

Answers to Questions About Spiritual Warfare

In the spiritual life, troubling circumstances have a way of claiming our attention! But if we fail to view daily spiritual challenges against the big picture of spiritual warfare, we can draw wrong conclusions and implement ineffective strategies. *Answers to Questions About Spiritual Warfare* addresses both Satan's strategies against the human race and the believer's strategies for defense and victory in spiritual battles. From his years of teaching on this subject, Pastor David Jeremiah has selected answers to every pertinent question concerning victory in the spiritual realm.

Understanding the 66 Books of the Bible

The Bible is the mind of Christ between two covers; but those covers enclose 66 books that may seem confusing. But the Lord imparted His Word to teach us, not baffle us; and each of His 66 books is understandable and vital to our well-being. In *Understanding the 66 Books of the Bible,* each book of the Bible, from Genesis to Revelation, is explained in an easy-to-understand way. Key thoughts, verses, actions, and prayers are included for each book to provide insight on familiar, or not-so-familiar, passages, taking us on a quick journey through God's Word.

STAY CONNECTED
TO DR. DAVID JEREMIAH

Take advantage of two great ways to let Dr. David Jeremiah give you spiritual direction every day! Both are absolutely FREE.

Turning Points Magazine and Devotional

Receive Dr. David Jeremiah's magazine, *Turning Points* each month:

- Thematic study focus
- 48 pages of life-changing reading
- Relevant articles
- Special features
- Daily devotional readings
- Bible study resource offers
- Live event schedule
- Radio & television information

Daily Turning Point E-Devotional

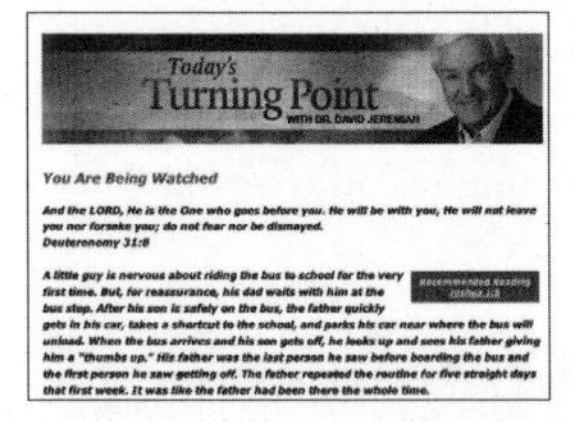

Today's Turning Point WITH DR. DAVID JEREMIAH

You Are Being Watched

And the LORD, He is the One who goes before you. He will be with you, He will not leave you nor forsake you; do not fear nor be dismayed.
Deuteronomy 31:8

A little guy is nervous about riding the bus to school for the very first time. But, for reassurance, his dad waits with him at the bus stop. After his son is safely on the bus, the father quickly gets in his car, takes a shortcut to the school, and parks his car near where the bus will unload. When the bus arrives and his son gets off, he looks up and sees his father giving him a "thumbs up." His father was the last person he saw before boarding the bus and the first person he saw getting off. The father repeated the routine for five straight days that first week. It was like the father had been there the whole time.

Start your day off right! Find words of inspiration and spiritual motivation waiting for you on your computer every morning! Receive a daily e-devotion communication from David Jeremiah that will strengthen your walk with God and encourage you to live the authentic Christian life.

There are two easy ways to sign up for these free resources from Turning Point. Visit us online at www.DavidJeremiah.org and select "Subscribe to Daily Devotional by Email" or visit the home page and find Daily Devotional to subscribe to your monthly copy of *Turning Points*.